PUSH ⦿ ONCE

-life in the bus industry

Peter Nash

Published by Kithead Limited, 2013

Printed by Gomer Press Ltd Llandysul

This book is dedicated to the man on the Clapham Omnibus,
who ultimately pays our wages

As Author I am grateful to the many people who have provided the pictures. Don Akrigg, Nigel Barrett, Ron Barton, Alan Cannell, David Cole, David Clark, Brian Cox, Trevor Hall, Andy Izatt, Ken Jubb, Malcolm Keeley, John Laker, Alan Millar, Richard Morant, Gary Nolan, Howard Piltz, John Senior, Ray Stenning, Ken Swallow, Andrew Thompson, David Thrower, Julian Walker, Michael Waller, Mark Watson, John Young and Tony Young have also willingly supplied images from their personal collections. Malcolm Crowe and Jim Whiting deserve special mention for taking pictures "to order". I am also grateful to another individual who has both provided images and assisted in their processing but wishes to remain anonymous. Peter Jaques has proof-read the text and offered invaluable guidance and support throughout. All have done so willingly and without recompense; a magnificent response for a worthy cause. Finally, John Senior has taken manuscript, captions and images and skilfully designed the book you are now reading, splicing in additional pictures from his own collection to fill gaps and enhance the story in some chapters. I sincerely thank them all and hope you enjoy reading this book as much as I have enjoyed writing it. Any profits will be donated to the Kithead Trust, a national archive for the bus industry.

ISBN 978-1-872863-14-6

Published by Kithead Ltd, De Salis Drive, Hampton Lovett, Droitwich, WR9 0QE

Sole distributors: MDS Booksales 128 Pikes Lane Glossop SK13 8EH
01457 861508 email: orders@mdsbooks.co.uk website: www.mdsbooks.co.uk

CONTENTS

About the Author   *Inside front cover*

Acknowledgements   2

Introduction   4

Foreword   6

Made in Birmingham   8

Beside the Seaside   12

There's Only One United   15

The Friendly Midland Red   21

The little Company with the big heart   30

Tales from the West Riding   35

Express Services   41

Time for Change – the 1968 Transport Act   49

Pay Day   61

Tales from the platform   64

Long Service   71

Stop Thief!   74

Service with a smile   79

From the Union Office   87

Who's in Charge?   91

Take Me to the Metrocentre   94

That's Preposterous!   97

Destination Displays   99

Ptegasaurus   101

London's Different   105

The View from North of the Border   111

The Warm Heart of Africa   117

Buggy Wars   122

Royal Visits   124

The Bare Cheeked Mayor
and the Clock that Stopped at Midnight   127

Three Close Calls   132

Going for Gold   136

Time to Say Goodbye   142

And finally . . . Model Buses   144

About the Kithead Trust   *Inside rear cover*

INTRODUCTION

During my bus industry career I was privileged to work for six very different employers. Each business had its own unique culture determined by its past, the way it organized itself and the vision, autonomy and capability of its management. I soon came to realize that the quality of service delivered to our customers is as much a product of the regard in which we hold our paymasters as the policies and procedures they seek to implement. As Bob Diamond, former CEO of Barclays Bank neatly put it, "corporate culture is how people behave when no one is watching them."

Throughout those 46 years I was lucky enough to meet and work with some talented, professional people, and yes, there were a few plonkers too. The vast majority, however, were wholly dedicated to the industry and to the ultimate goal of getting passengers to their destinations, whatever the circumstances and sometimes despite the prevailing culture. No matter what job we do, this is the glue which binds us all together. I was once told that if you could survive the first two years in the business, then derv would permeate your blood and you would catch the busmen's disease – a career on the buses. If, like me, you can't resist a glance at every passing bus to see how many passengers it is carrying, then you have definitely contracted the virus.

Speak to anyone who has worked in the industry for a while and they will be able to tell you stories. Tales of things that should have happened but didn't, or things that shouldn't have happened but did. It is inevitable that in a people business like ours, there will be some occasions when human weakness gets the upper hand. I was therefore determined to capture the spirit of our industry and present it in this publication for everyone to share. I am grateful for the many contributions and illustrations from colleagues and acquaintances which together have enabled me to paint this "warts and all" picture of our industry as it has evolved and changed over the past fifty years.

Wherever you look, today's bus industry is very different from that of the 1960s. Methods of working, marketing, communications, fares collection, the vehicles and their technologies: you name it, it has changed, sometimes beyond recognition. The only constant is the commitment of the people who work in the bus business.

This publication is the result of the collaborative efforts of some fifty people. My call for contributions was willingly answered by over thirty busmen, nearly all of whom have dedicated their working lives to the British bus industry. Several of them gave freely of their time to be interviewed by me, and many conducted further research to verify their recollections and provided valuable images to illustrate their stories. They are all named in the text and each has provided one or more unique pieces of the jigsaw which together paint a colourful picture of life on the buses as it has changed over the last half century.

So push the bell twice and enjoy the ride!

Peter Nash

There is no place for a revenue protection squad on Manchester city centre's free Metroshuttle buses. Would Les Burton miss the challenge? Read about his experiences on page 75. (John Senior)

FOREWORD

BY SIR BRIAN SOUTER

Looking back over my time in the bus industry, a lot has changed. We are moving from paper tickets to smartcards and mobile ticketing. Where once we had fixed turn-up-and-go fares, we now have flexible pricing and online booking and new state-of-the-art green hybrid-electric buses are taking over from the traditional combustion engine.

But in amongst all this change there is one constant – it's the people that make buses and coaches a great and exciting industry. I've come across some real characters over the years – several of them are mentioned in this book. The best of them have been ones with good ideas, who can build relationships and work in partnership to achieve things.

It's a bit ironic that in 2013, there is still a pointless debate about regulation, structures and control when it is people, partnerships and good products at attractive prices that make people choose to leave their car and catch the bus. I'm very fortunate that I'm doing a job I love. At college, I got a job as a bus conductor on Saturdays and in the holidays. Nearly four decades later, I'm still getting a buzz out of running Stagecoach. I saw buses as an exciting opportunity, but without my father, Iain, and a number of other people along the way, Stagecoach wouldn't exist as it is. My dad put his life savings into Stagecoach in the early days and had real confidence in the company. You should also never be too proud to surround yourself with people who are better and brighter than you – that's how many a good business has become successful.

In the early days in Glasgow, I remember doing split shifts and going to university lectures with my uniform on. I was stared at by students who all wore denims – they thought I was a crazy union shop steward who was trying to better himself!

"... it is people, partnerships and good products at attractive prices that make people choose to leave their car and catch the bus." A tri-axle Scania Megabus awaits the return of its passengers after a short-duration comfort and refreshment stop, when arriving early for a driver changeover on the northbound M1. (John Senior)

At Stagecoach, we've always been a bit different. That means you can attract a fair bit of attention at times! We've grown dramatically over the years and we've run transport operations in five continents but we've still remained true to our culture and our convictions. We have a small but very effective team of senior managers and only a few links in the chain from the Chief Executive to the driver on the bus. I still enjoy doing a driving shift at one of our companies every year. Last summer, I was also proud to get a chance to get behind the wheel and be part of a great team of more than 2,600 Stagecoach bus drivers and support staff that played an important part in delivering public transport for the London 2012 Olympic and Paralympic Games. We have a great group of people and we're happy working together.

Reading some of the anecdotes in Peter's book has certainly brought back a few memories about the old days and the adventures, battles and scrapes we've had along the way. You could fill many a book with such stories. But, in celebrating the past, I also have confidence that the future of Stagecoach and the wider bus industry in Britain is in good hands. There are some very talented young managers coming through, full of ideas and enthusiasm.

Some people might think of buses as out-dated, but I think it's an exciting time. Interestingly, buses will be seen as the natural and sustainable way of getting around. We're already starting to change how people think about bus travel. The business opportunities are still there – our budget coach service megabus.com is getting the same kind of amazing response as our first coach services from Scotland to London had in the early 1980s.

I hope you enjoy reading these fascinating and funny recollections about life on the buses. Profits will go to the Kithead Trust, an educational charity that is helping preserve a rich library of important documents about the industry that would otherwise be lost to history. I'm sure there are many more chapters of our industry's great story still to be written in the future.

Brian Souter

MADE IN BIRMINGHAM

Midland Red, or to give it its full title, The Birmingham and Midland Motor Omnibus Company Limited, (BMMO) was the last British bus operator to build its own vehicles. Between 1923 and 1969, BMMO built the chassis of most of the buses it operated and some were supplied to other BET subsidiary Companies. From 1954 it built most of the bodies as well. One particular man, Loftus George Wyndham Shire, the visionary Chief Engineer, had created the production capability and was responsible for the SOS chassis which were built in the company's Carlyle workshops in Birmingham. There were all sorts of suggestions as to what SOS stood for and Shire himself was always very evasive about it. However a patent application signed by Shire in 1924 refers to "Superior Omnibus Specification" which seems to put the matter beyond doubt.

It was said that Shire would inspect each vehicle before delivery and that on one occasion he was so displeased with the result that he walked down the side of the bus and smashed the windows with his walking cane as he went. Whether true or not, the pre-war BMMO Company was certainly run on unconventional lines and Wyndham Shire was matched by an equally larger than life Traffic Manager, Orlando Cecil Power. After 1928, there was no General Manager to hold the ring and with drivers responsible to Shire and conductors to Power, each man ran his own empire and barely communicated with the other. They were both based in the same head office building at Bearwood, but there was a locked door between the two departments, the key to which was held by their go-between the Staff Manager, who headed a third Midland Red department. Unfortunately, Shire's inflexibility, arguably a strength in peacetime, left him unable to cope with the additional challenges of wartime problems and he was asked to retire, leaving the company in June 1940 and being replaced by Donald Sinclair from Northern. Power unexpectedly died in service in 1943, which cleared the way for Midland Red to adopt the more conventional management structure adopted by other British bus operators, by appointing Sinclair as General Manager, who then held both positions until S.C. Vince was appointed Chief Engineer in 1946.

Midland Red designed buses were technically advanced but best described as functional in

L.G. Wyndham Shire was a man who demanded the highest standards from his staff and who was the driving force behind Midland Red's bus production. (BMMO, courtesy The Transport Museum ,Wythall)

appearance. Many built in the 1950s and 1960s were characterised by a flat sloping driver's windscreen which minimized internal reflections at night. This feature was common to nearly every vehicle design, but while distinctive, it could hardly be called pleasing to the eye. Even "bought in" buses like the LS18 Leyland Leopard single deckers with either Weymann or Willowbrook bodies, or the LD8 double-decks were specified with sloping screens.

The LD8 vehicles were a batch of 100 all-Leyland 56-seat Titan PD2s with rear platform doors, the first of which was delivered in 1952. It was inevitable, given Midland Red's bus building expertise, that the vehicles would be customized to Midland Red's requirements. The specification included the inevitable sloping driver's windscreen and an enclosed radiator, as was common on all post-1944 Midland Red vehicles. Midland Red designed a twelve slat radiator grille with space at the top for a BMMO logo. Leyland subsequently adopted this grille for use on its Leyland Titan PD2/20 models, which were sold in large numbers nationwide.

The last Midland Red double-decker to be built in numbers was the D9 and for once this was a handsome vehicle. In part this was because it was the only Midland Red built post-war bus with a vertical driver's windscreen. The first prototype was built in 1958 and 344 more followed between 1960 and 1966 but the last 45 had to be completed by Willowbrook owing to skills shortages at Carlyle Works. Many have

said that the D9 was Midland Red's answer to London's Routemaster and the production run spanned a similar period – 1960 to 1966. The D9 was 30 ft long, taking advantage of the 1956 legislation permitting double-deckers of this length, unlike London's shorter RM but the same as the later RML which has an extra body section added to capitalize on the new maximum length. For the technically minded, the D9 was fitted with a front-mounted 10½-litre BMMO KL engine, hydraulically operated four-speed semi-automatic CAV gearbox, disc-brakes on both axles and power steering. The front axle was independently sprung and variable rate rubber suspension was used throughout. The body was of fully integral half-cab construction made from aluminium alloy, with the roof, front end, staircase, rear dome and other smaller parts made of fibreglass. The doors were electrically operated, mounted on the rear platform and the vehicle seated a total of seventy-two, the same as London's RML. Visually, the most striking part of the D9's appearance was the short wheelbase at just over 17 ft with large overhangs at the front and rear thus enabling a tight turning circle.

With its power steering, the D9 was a driver's bus, but the original disc brakes overheated and had to be replaced by drums and these were not ideal by modern standards. The Metalastik rubber suspension, however, made for an impressive ride when laden. Unfortunately, when hitting a pothole unladen the vehicle tended to bounce down the road

Midland Red built 218 S14 single-deckers between 1955 and 1959. Designed for rural operations, these four wheel integral buses were powered by an underfloor BMMO 8-litre engine and weighed a little over 5 tonnes unladen. This 43-seat example, seen loading in Bridgnorth, was one of the third and final batch constructed. (Geoffrey Morant)

like a kangaroo – much to the chagrin of many a conductor who was trying to cash up on the back seat as the driver floored the throttle on the last run back to the garage.

I well remember one particular Saturday in 1970 when I was driving a D9 on the 118 Birmingham-Walsall service, by then jointly operated with Walsall Corporation. There was no need for either operator to worry about schedules efficiency, since once outside the watchful eyes of the bus station inspectors at either end, the name of the game was to try and narrow the gap with the bus in front, thus sparing your conductor any additional workload. On the day concerned, we were completing our run into Birmingham a minute or two early when as I slowed to enter Birmingham Bull Ring bus station I applied the footbrake to no effect. I managed to steer the vehicle into the correct lane and pulled the hand brake on as hard as I could. Luckily, there were no buses standing in the outside lane, as was often the case. We glided down the lane, past the 118 pick-up stop and eventually came to rest some 20 metres further on. Passengers came round to the front to remonstrate with me about missing the stop and once they had had their say my conductor asked what the problem was, to which I replied "no brakes". I went in

Seen here at Carlyle Works, prototype BMMO D9 72-seat double-decker 4773 has yet to have its BMMO badge fitted. This was the first of 345 D9s, the last of which was completed in 1966. 4773 entered service in February 1959 and spent its entire working life at Sheepcote Street Garage in Birmingham until July 1972 when it was sold for preservation. Also pictured is a 56-seat Brush bodied BMMO D5B, one of 100 built between 1950 and 1952. (BMMO, courtesy The Transport Museum ,Wythall)

Below: The rear view of 5424, finished by Willowbrook in 1966 and now also preserved, shows the long rear overhang and rear platform door arrangement, with emergency exit. The brightwork enhances its appearance. (John Senior)

search of the duty mechanic, whose job it was to keep the fleet rolling with any minor repairs. When I explained my predicament he looked me up and down and came out with a classic reply which I shall never forget: "can't you do another trip, mate?" Needless to say he had to convince himself that the bus was unserviceable before he somewhat grudgingly gave me his only spare vehicle, an elderly D7, to complete my shift. I later broke into a sweat when I contemplated what might have happened if my brakes had failed ten minutes earlier as I had sped down the Walsall Road into Birmingham. Intrigued, I later made it my business to discover the cause of the brake failure. It transpired that a sharp object (probably thrown up by one of the wheels) had penetrated one of the armoured flexible brake hoses attached to the front brakes, which meant that every depression of

the brake merely resulted in a jet of brake fluid through the fracture.

Building your own vehicles meant that you could design buses and coaches specifically for your own requirements. Midland Red did this to great effect and was able to grab the national headlines with its CM5 and CM6 coaches, which it had specially designed for motorway work – this in the days before national speed limits but more of this later.

Just as London Transport experimented with its front-entrance Routemaster so did Midland Red with an underfloor engined front-entrance double-decker. This was the D10 and only two such vehicles were built, the first of which took to the road in January 1961. The problem with mounting the engine under the floor of double-deck vehicles is one of maintaining head room within the overall height. This was solved by using a specially modified version of the BMMO 10½-litre engine mounted horizontally on the nearside with the cylinder heads facing towards the centre of the bus and the crankcase towards the outside. As a result, the protruding flywheel housing was clear of the lower-deck gangway and headroom of 5ft 11¼in (1.81m) was achieved on the lower deck and 5ft 9¼in (1.76m) on the upper-deck, all within an overall vehicle height of 14ft 4½in (4.38m). Pretty much all of the other parts were common with the standard D9. The second prototype was more unusual than the first, having two staircases, on the theory that passengers would board at the front and alight at the rear. This vehicle only had 65 seats and 18 months of operational tests went sufficiently badly that it was soon returned to the Works to be re-configured conventionally like its sister.

With a potential 78-seat payload these buses had traffic department approval, but the off-centre engine mounting created uneven weight distribution and uneven wear on brake and suspension components. The angled drive-train reduced power to the wheels, consuming more fuel, while the engine location compromised the integrity of the frame leading to cracks in stress panels in later life. The option to discontinue D9 construction and to switch to D10s was not therefore taken up. There were also clouds gathering over the Carlyle Works facility and its production capacity. These were exacerbated by the loss of skilled staff to the (then) booming car manufacture plant at Longbridge a few miles away. The fact that Midland Red had insufficient labour to complete the last batch of D9's was testament enough to its difficulties. So, in 1961, the decision was made to run down production capability at Carlyle Works and the next batches of new buses were bought in. These included 100 "off the shelf" Leyland Leopard LS18 single-deckers in 1962, (the first of 550 Leopards to be purchased before

Seen in Stafford, this is the first of two prototype underfloor-engined Midland Red D10s. By the late 1960s the MIDLAND logo had been replaced with the script 'Midland Red', originally reserved for coaches and semi-coaches. Also visible is a 1960 Potteries Motor Traction 73-seat Weymann bodied Leyland Atlantean PDR1/1 laying over before returning to Newcastle-under-Lyme. 4943 entered service in 1961 and is preserved at the Transport Museum, Wythall. (Geoffrey Morant)

the Company's eventual demise in 1981) and in 1963 the first of 340 D11, D12, D13 and D14 Daimler Fleetlines with Alexander bodies suitable for one-person operation were purchased. Finally, the two D10s were put out to grass at Stafford garage from which they operated until the last was finally withdrawn in January 1973.

Despite the decision to reduce production at Carlyle, the Works delivered the S17 single-decker in 1963 and 1964, and the S21 in 1967 and then from 1968 to 1970, the S22 and S23 single-deckers. I was fortunate enough to be there in January 1970 when the very last entirely Midland Red built vehicle, S23 number 5941 (UHA 941H), was completed, the handover date being delayed for a week so that it could coincide with a ceremony to mark the date on which George Bill, the Carlyle Works Superintendent reached 50 years service with the Company. This man, who had been responsible for supervising bus construction, retired at the end of March the following year having been there when every Midland Red bus ever built had left Carlyle Works, the true end of an era for both the man and his buses. While there was a further 50 S23s, these were completed by Plaxtons, because of Midland Red staff shortages.

In January 1970, George Bill, the Carlyle Works Superintendent, completed fifty years service with Midland Red. He is seen here at the handover of the last bus fully completed at Carlyle, 51-seat S23, 5941. (BMMO, courtesy Kithead Trust)

BESIDE THE SEASIDE

For much of the post war period before 1970, the vast majority of English company bus services were operated by two major transport groups, one of which comprised the Tilling Companies which were nationalized in 1948. They became part of the Transport Holding Company (THC) in 1962 as a consequence of the Transport Act of that year. These included famous names such as Bristol Omnibus, Crosville, Eastern Counties, Hants & Dorset, Southern National, Thames Valley, United Automobile and Western National. These fleets were largely made up of Eastern Coach Works-bodied Bristol vehicles, which had also become part of the nationalised THC portfolio and whose vehicles the Companies were required to purchase. The predominant livery tended to be all-over green, but there were red examples too, like Brighton Hove & District, Cheltenham & District, Thames Valley, West Yorkshire, Wilts & Dorset and United, and even some blue ones like Midland General.

The other major grouping was the British Electric Traction Co. Ltd (BET). In 1967, its subsidiaries ran some 12,000 buses, employed 50,000 staff and had a gross turnover of £70 million. The BET portfolio included names like East Kent, Midland Red, Northern, Oxford,

A Bristol RE with ECW body from the Eastern Counties fleet, seen in Norwich in 1972, typifies single-deck vehicles from the former Tilling fleets which would pass to the NBC. (John Senior)

This is one of nine Roe-bodied Leyland Atlantean PDR1/1s built to a Park Royal 75-seat design and with detachable roofs. It was delivered to Devon General in 1961 where it remained until 1982. Each bus was named after a famous admiral earning them their Sea Dog nicknames. (Roy Marshall)

Potteries, Ribble, Southdown and Trent. Their liveries tended to be more imaginative with the use of a wide variety of colours and some attractive two-shaded liveries like Southdown. BET Companies remained in the private sector until BET announced on 22nd November 1967 that it had agreed to sell its shares to the Transport Holding Company for £35 million. The announcement came as a surprise to many, particularly as BET had mounted a publicity campaign opposing nationalisation, but secret negotiations had been going on for some months using the code name "TOMATOES". Thus, virtually the entire industry was now in public ownership of one sort or another and the Government was able to create the National Bus Company (NBC) out of the assets it then owned and include provision for it in the Transport Bill which was published 15 days later. NBC took legal responsibility for the bus operations of the Transport Holding Company as from 1st January 1969.

Before this merger, the two groups gave their managements very different levels of local autonomy. There was more central policy control in the THC Companies than in BET Companies, where the General Manager had wide discretion to run his business as he chose, answerable only to his Directors at BET headquarters at Stratton House in Piccadilly, London.

One typical BET company was Devon General where Peter Shipp joined the industry as a Traffic Apprentice. When Peter arrived, his General Manager, Tom Strange, who

could be a demanding individual, had recently purchased a fleet of nine new 75-seat Leyland Atlanteans with removable roofs for use on the popular open-top services. The vehicles were nicknamed the "Sea Dogs" each being named after a famous British sailor. Peter recalls a depot walkabout where Strange had inspected the vehicles and had run his finger round the window pans and then loudly admonished the engineers because "his buses were dirty!" He also became annoyed if he saw any buses in the depot over the evening peak period, since they should all have been out "earning money". Whether he realised that the engineering staff would have nothing to do at 4pm if there were no vehicles to maintain, unless there was a radical change to their shift patterns, seems unlikely.

Before 1981, all operators outside London had to apply to the Traffic Commissioner (TC) if they wanted to increase fares, since, under the 1930 Road Traffic Act, the TC regulated both fares and services. In order to justify a fares increase it was necessary to produce the company accounts and schedules of anticipated expenditure and fares yields, and Local Authorities could object to the Company's proposals if they wished. Peter recalls attending one such Public Inquiry where Devon General's

Over 8000 AEC Reliance chassis were produced for home and overseas markets between 1954 and 1972. Laying over in Paignton, after a 1963 summer shower, was one of a 1957 batch of 14 with Weymann 41-seat bodywork. (Geoffrey Morant)

Traffic Manager, Len Crook, was explaining to the TC that the company had experienced a poor summer because it had been so hot that people had spent the whole day on the beach, rather than ride around on the buses. The TC, Samuel Gibbon, pondered for a moment and then said "I remember you telling me last year, Mr Crook, that you had had a poor summer because it had rained too much. Can you please tell me just what sort of weather does suit your Company?"

Peter remembers another Public Inquiry for a fares increase in the Exeter area, which was attended by Messrs Strange and Crook, Peter having been invited along for the experience. The increase having been granted, they had all climbed into the General Manager's black Austin Westminster to return to Torquay, although Peter noticed that they had diverted off route via Chudleigh, where they stopped for lunch. When 3pm came, the publican shut the curtains and the two managers continued to

consume large amounts of alcohol. At one stage Tom Strange asked Peter to go and look for Len Crook's false teeth which he had apparently lost in the loo. Peter duly searched and found them submerged in the urinal and therefore decided to report back that he couldn't see them – leaving Len Crook to recover them himself. 4pm came and Tom Strange handed Peter the car keys with the words "I think you had better have these". Peter chauffeured his two less than sober passengers back to Torquay and dropped Len Crook off at his home in Kingskerswell. To deliver Tom Strange to his front door, Peter needed to pass the Head Office and as they approached, Tom tapped Peter on the shoulder and indicated that he wished to be dropped off at the office. Peter could only conclude that he didn't dare go home in the condition he was in and needed to sober up before doing so. Quite how he got there, Peter didn't know as he had custody of the Austin Westminster until the following morning!

New in 1959, and seen here in Vaughan Parade, Torquay, this was the last of Devon General's first batch of 17 Leyland Atlantean PDR1/1s. The Metro-Cammell-built body provided 78 seats but the later addition of a nearside luggage pen reduced this to 76. (Geoffrey Morant)

THERE'S ONLY ONE UNITED

At the opposite end of England from Devon General was the United Company. Whenever Newcastle United Football Club plays Manchester United the chant of "There's only one United" rings out from St James Park, just across the road from the site of Newcastle's once famous Gallowgate Coach Station. But, so far as the bus industry is concerned, there were once two Uniteds.

United Automobile Services Limited was founded in Suffolk by the noted entrepreneur E.B. Hutchinson in 1912. Unusually for a developing bus operator, the Company created two bases some 275 miles apart, one at Lowestoft and the other in County Durham, where the first service ran between Bishop Auckland and Durham. The 1920s brought rapid expansion from both bases, so that the Company soon had operations from Berwick-upon-Tweed on the Scottish border through Northumberland and Durham to North Yorkshire, and from Lincolnshire to Norfolk and Suffolk.

Territorially this made United one of the two most widespread bus operating companies

in Great Britain at that time. Hutchinson eventually sold out to Tilling & British Automobile Co. Ltd, the holding company jointly owned by Tillings and the BET in 1929. This led to a restructuring of the business two years later when the East Anglian operations were separated and rebranded as Eastern Counties. The now smaller United, with its Head Office in Darlington, still served a huge area from Berwick to Scarborough some 150 miles further south and, apart from Northern and the municipal fleets, it was the principal bus operator serving the counties of Northumberland, Durham and North Yorkshire. With such a large geographic spread it is no surprise that the Company appointed some charismatic individuals, including one A.T. Evans, to run its diverse business.

Newcastle's Gallowgate Coach Station in April 1984 with a 73-seat MCW Metroliner awaiting departure on National Express Rapide service 525 to London Victoria. Behind lies Tyne and Wear Metro's St James terminus and the Gallowgate end of St James Park football ground, before its redevelopment. This coach was written off after overturning on the A1(M) in a fatal accident in August 1985. (Mark Watson)

1965 mid-weight ECW-bodied Bristol MWs with 5 or 6 cylinder Gardner engines were built between 1957 and 1967. This immaculate 45-seat example, laying over at Belford in 1965, is one of 283 MWs delivered to United. (Geoffrey Morant)

A.T. Evans was a colourful character who rose to become General Manager of United in the 1950s. In pre-war years, United had consolidated its position by acquiring the more successful independent operators in its area but Evans was astute enough to realise that some ran businesses which were never going to make a profit at United's cost levels. Despite approaches from many of the families who ran these operations and who were wanting to cash in their investments, he would decline their enquiries on the basis that it was better that they, and not United, were politically pressured to keep their services running. When questioned by David Deacon, his then Traffic Manager, he summed up his strategy with the words "We don't want that trash, son".

Originally registered HHN 213, this vehicle started life as a Bristol L5G half-cab 35-seat single-deck bus in 1947. It was rebodied by ECW with 39 seats in 1957 when it was lengthened to 30 ft. Clearly desgned for this promenade work the vehicles were fitted with glass cantrails for improved visibility, and additional destinations equipment amidships. United would not have been alone in finding that in bright summer sunshine the glass cantrails could have been a mixed blessing. It is seen here working the Scarborough sea front service, with a full standing load and more potential passengers hoping to board. (Geoffrey Morant)

This 1950-built Bristol L5G keeps alive the memory of the United company and its famous Bristol single-deckers. Rebuilt in later life to a more mundane front-entrance layout than the example opposite, to enable it to be used for one-person-operation, it is now well-known as one of the stars in the popular TV series Heartbeat. Here it is working at the Beamish open air museum in County Durham. (John Senior)

This 78-seat ECW bodied Bristol FLF6L is climbing out of Bishop Auckland in August 1972 on the route of United's first service in the north-east of England sixty years earlier. Between 1949 and 1968, Bristol produced over 5200 Lodekka chassis which employed a drop-centre rear axle to enable upper saloon two-by-two seating within a low overall height (13ft 6in or 4.12m). (Roy Marshall)

Taffy Evans, as he was called behind his back, abused and charmed his staff in equal measure. He would often arrive unannounced to inspect the Company's operations driven by his chauffeur and accompanied by his Labrador dog. After one such visit to Whitby, the staff were relieved that they had successfully passed muster but later that afternoon the bus station Inspector found a stray Labrador roaming the premises. Using his initiative, he seized his opportunity to make his mark with the boss. He collected an O.C.S. [On Company's Service] label from the office, wrote on it "A. T. Evans Darlington", tied it round the animal's neck, found a piece of twine to act as a makeshift lead and despatched the dog on the next bus to Middlesbrough. After a self-congratulatory cup of tea, he rang Darlington to inform them that the dog was on its way, only to be told by the telephonist that Evans and his dog had just walked in.

Another United stalwart was Havelock Farrer who for many years managed the Company's Northumberland operations from his office in Gallowgate Coach Station, Newcastle. As Area Traffic Superintendent he had responsibility for over 450 buses operating from nine depots and also the Ashington-Newcastle-London express coach services which glided up and down the A1 three times a day. When Havelock retired in 1975, such was the high regard in which he was held that the Newcastle Civic Centre banqueting suite was full to bursting with colleagues past and present from both United and many other operators in the North East who wanted to mark his retirement. When it came to the speeches, Havelock gave an entertaining review of his career and in doing so didn't pull any punches.

Havelock told one story which, for me, summed up the uneasy relationship which often exists between Traffic and Engineering staff at depot level in many places. It is an inevitable consequence of their differing objectives that there would occasionally be tension between the two. Traffic staff would regard themselves to be somewhat superior as they didn't get

New in August 1980, this 74-seat ECW-bodied Bristol VRT/SL3 was transferred to Northumbria Motor Services when United was split prior to privatization in 1986. It is loading in North Shields in June 1993 and displays Northumbria's striking livery. Northumbria's owners, Proudmutual, sold out to the Sunderland based Cowie Group the following year and Cowie purchased the rest of United two years later. In 1997 the group was renamed Arriva. (Roy Marshall)

their hands dirty. Further, it was they who earned the money to keep the engineers in employment, whereas the engineers would often despair at the way drivers would treat "their" vehicles. One couldn't help feeling that some engineers would have preferred the fleet to remain safely tucked up in the depot rather than to be let loose on the highway where buses might break down or kamikaze drivers might collide with anything which got in their way. The tension was at its greatest when the daily run out took place and Traffic staff would be twitching as to whether or not the Engineers could produce enough buses to "make service". Havelock summed up this friction beautifully with this tale from his earlier days.

Scarborough is one of those resorts which used to overflow with visitors from Yorkshire, Teesside and the North East in the summer season. Havelock was then Traffic Superintendent in the town and responsible for running the sea-front services which regularly plied between the North Bay and the South Bay in the early 1950s, as they still do today. Havelock told the assembled gathering that if the weather was good, the service was a gold mine. All you had to do was get the buses out there. Therein lay his problem, because not one of the allocated vehicles was available for service at 8.30am on one glorious sunny morning in August. Havelock went to see his Engineering colleague to be treated to a catalogue of woes, but nevertheless with a fair wind he thought he might have something available for service within the hour – and would Havelock please now leave him to get on with things. By 9.30am Havelock knew that the holiday makers would have finished their breakfasts and be heading for the sea front in search of his open-toppers. Twenty past nine came and still no buses for service. Havelock had drivers, conductors and intending passengers but nothing to carry them on.

Another consultation with the Engineers took place. It would be ten minutes and the first bus would be ready – which was something of a relief as the crowds on the seafront were beginning to build up. True to their word the Engineers declared the first bus fit for service but there was one small snag – it wouldn't start. The United depot in Scarborough was on a hill and it was a straightforward downhill run to the seafront so the Engineers pushed the vehicle through the garage doors and the driver was instructed that once it was rolling he should drop it into gear as he gathered speed down the hill, and, under no circumstances

was he to switch the engine off. So off he went following his instructions to the letter. On arrival at the bottom of the hill, his bus still hadn't started, despite three attempts to drop it into gear on the way down. Now the situation was becoming critical. There was a driver, a conductor a bus and a very expectant queue of waiting passengers who could now see the object of their desire. Havelock concluded his story with these memorable words, "And do you know what the problem was? They hadn't reconnected the fuel tank!"

Until the formation of NBC in 1968, United was a typical Tilling company, the most obvious manifestation of which was its fleet of Bristol chassis with Eastern Coach Works (ECW) bodies, both manufacturers having been nationalized as part of the Tilling group in 1948. The ECW business was based in Lowestoft and originated from United's coach building workshops in the town.

With NBC came extra layers of management above the General Manager, including Regional Directors, and at various stages, Chief General Managers and Regional Executives. Neil Renilson recalls his days as a senior management trainee at United's Darlington head office, which was close to the regional office inhabited by NBC's Northern Region Director (RD). One day he was asked if he could drive the Regional Director and his General Manager to Wakefield for a long-service presentation at the West Riding Company. The event was on a Saturday night and the RD's chauffeur didn't work weekends. Neil readily agreed, particularly as he fancied the opportunity to put the RD's Jaguar through its paces on the nearby M1 motorway. The journey south was uneventful and he deposited his distinguished passengers at the venue with instructions to return by 11pm to take them back north.

Neil enjoyed stretching the Jaguar's legs on a virtually deserted motorway and duly returned to collect his passengers. He noted that both seemed a little the worse for wear as they set off back to Darlington some 75 miles north. It was around 1am when they reached the outskirts of the town and the General Manager asked if he could be dropped off first. First stop completed, Neil noted in his mirror that the RD was now asleep, but as he knew where he lived he thought no more of it. He stopped outside the RD's house and, as he was still asleep, went up the path and rang the front door bell. The house was in darkness and remained so until on the third ring of the bell a light appeared on the first floor. Neil returned to the car and somehow managed to carry/guide his RD to the front door where he propped him against the door post. Satisfied that someone was coming downstairs, he then beat a hasty retreat and returned the car to the nearby United depot. Job well done, he thought.

On the following Monday morning Neil went into work as usual, to be told on arrival that the General Manager wanted to see him. Strange, thought Neil, perhaps he just wants to compliment me on my Saturday night's chauffeuring duties. He knocked on the GM's door and when told to "enter" he was surprised to be greeted with "Don't sit down Renilson. This won't take long". What had he done? The GM continued, "If you want to get on in this business, young man, you are going to have to pay much more attention to detail." Neil was still none the wiser, but all was revealed when his GM said, "You should be aware that the Regional Director lives at number 37, not number 39."

The 1985 Transport Act required that United, like every other NBC Company, should be privatized. The Secretary of State took the view that some larger NBC Companies would have an unfair competitive advantage if they were sold as one, so he issued a Direction in February 1986 that United, along with Ribble, Crosville and London Country should be split before privatization took place. Thus in

United's case, the Northumberland operations which were once Havelock Farrer's empire, became a separate Company. United's Durham and North Yorkshire operations were sold to Caldaire Holdings, the company formed by the management buy-out team at West Riding, and the Northumberland operations were bought by Proudmutual, led by three of the incumbent United management team. However, through a series of sales in the 1990s, the two businesses were eventually reunited under common ownership, which today is the Arriva UK business, now owned by Deutsche Bahn.

So the United wheel has come full circle, the business covers largely the same territory as it did in 1931 and once again it is part of a larger group of companies. It does have a different trading name and is also back in state ownership as it was from 1948 to 1986, albeit answering now to Berlin instead of Westminster.

Arriva Volvo B7TL with Alexander ALX 400 dual-purpose 72-seat body, sister vehicle to that featured on the front cover, has been cleverly rebranded to celebrate the United centenary in 2012 using a "zip" design first tested by Arriva in 2000 at Groningen in the Netherlands. This striking application of vinyl graphics has more visual impact than the "paint it like it was" treatment traditionally used to celebrate important milestones. (Trevor Hall)

THE FRIENDLY MIDLAND RED

While United was the largest ex-Tilling Group company, Midland Red was by far the largest of the BET companies. I joined the company in September 1969 as a Senior Management Trainee when it was entering its twilight years. The company ran over 1750 buses and coaches from 33 depots stretching across six counties. The General Manager, J. Walter Womar and his deputy, Derek Fytche, along with the Accountants, were based in Midland House, previously a home for unmarried mothers and their babies, at Vernon Road Edgbaston, which backed on to Carlyle Works, where the Company built and overhauled its buses. The Engineering Head Office was in the Works and the Traffic Offices were at Bearwood, a couple of miles away. Throughout the Midlands the company was known as the friendly Midland Red, the result of years of using the by-line in publicity materials. However, widespread staff shortages at that time had led to high levels of unreliability and I well recall seeing many a letter of complaint beginning with the words "I thought that you were the friendly Midland Red but....", which only goes to prove that if you over promise, it eventually comes back to bite you.

Walter Womar was more a business man than a busman. He liked to play the stock market and I recall towards the end of my two year training period, spending time at Midland House and being summoned to see him, to be told that there was a Canadian mining company called Barymin and he had received a tip that it was worth a punt. My task was to establish whether or not he should invest in it! My first port of call was the Company Accountant, Norman Rolfe, who acted as Womar's private stockbroker. There was no Google in those days, but he gave me some pointers as to how I might find the answer. I set off to Birmingham Central Library with a notebook in my pocket to try and gain an understanding of the Canadian minerals prospecting business. I quickly established that most of these mining businesses held shares in each other and I was advised that if I really needed to get to the bottom of the issue, I should visit the Canadian Embassy in London, which I did. There I managed to access a number of mining trade journals

This 1969 line up of Midland Red-built buses in Evesham comprises four S14s, (service number to the right), an S15 (black roof), two S17s and a D9 double-decker. The S15, with its dual-purpose defining black roof was an S14 derivative, but with double rear wheels, bucket seats, and luggage racks. 98 S15's were built and 5052 (HA 5052) came new to Evesham in 1961. The S17s (service number to the left) had bodywork finished by Plaxton or Willowbrook to the new 36ft maximum legal length. Powered by BMMO 10.5-litre engines, their semi-automatic gear changes appealed to drivers. (Photobus)

Midland Red took delivery of 350 D7's between 1953 and 1957. Built in four batches on BMMO chassis, with an improved BMMO KL engine and Metro-Cammell bodywork to BMMO specification, 4081 is an early example. The first batch had 58 seats, but top deck seating was later increased from 32 to 37. Despite passenger complaints about the reduction in legroom, later batches were built with 63 seats as standard. Photographed in Fisher Street Dudley, it sports permanent frontal advertisements for platform staff. It is working the busy Black Country 245 service known to crews as "the track", because it followed the route of the Dudley & Stourbridge tramway which closed in 1930.
(Roy Marshall)

which demonstrated that while Barymin wasn't itself likely to make an imminent discovery of new minerals, a Company in which it had a 25% stake probably would. I returned to Birmingham with my "buy" recommendation pondering why a bus management trainee should be tasked with investigating mineral prospecting, later reflecting that as initiative tests went, it was a fair challenge.

Womar set me another task during my time with him, which seemed more relevant to my training. The Company had recently implemented a fares increase and Womar was concerned that "the money isn't coming in" particularly at the Black Country garages. He was convinced that this was not because the Company had just implemented two large fares increases and that its passengers were voting with their feet, but because things were going wrong on the platform. I was given three days to produce a report about what was happening on the ground. I could immediately see that my findings from this particular challenge could make life difficult for Traffic Manager, James Isaac, but when I explained my task to him he was remarkably relaxed about it, even though the General Manager had not advised him of my exercise. James merely asked that I give him a confidential copy of my conclusions at the same time as I reported to Womar, so I set off for my two days of riding buses around the Black Country. As a trainee in such a large Company I was not known to the conductors and paid my fare as I went. I sat on the nearside rear bench seat so that I could observe what was happening in the lower saloon and on the platform with a good view of

the upper deck through the mirror. So what did I discover? Pretty much what would be found on most buses up and down the land. Not all the conductors charged me the correct fare, but the instances of over-charging were matched by the instances of under-charging. A lot of passengers were asking for their destination by fare, and so far as I could judge, some were asking for pre-increase fares values, which the conductors were challenging in about 90% of cases. I did observe one conductor "fiddling the tea money" by means of the time honoured dodge of collecting the fare on the platform from an alighting passenger, bagging the money and "forgetting" to issue a ticket. For this fiddle to work, timing was everything, as the passenger had to be more concerned about getting off the bus than collecting his ticket. What did surprise me, however, was the number of elderly passengers who were evading payment. In those days, Midland Red offered no discounts to the elderly and the fares were clearly hitting their meagre incomes. I later asked James Isaac whether the GM had raised my findings with him. He had, and James told me that he had explained that my conclusions were exactly what he would have expected!

A key element of the senior management training programme was securing your PSV licence and then gaining some on-the-road experience. I managed to get behind the wheel ahead of schedule, whilst with the Engineers at Wolverhampton early in my programme. The chief driving instructor there was a man by the name of Obe Grainger and he took me out in the converted C1 coach which had been relegated to driver training duties. These full-

Forty-five of these elegant full-fronted 30-seat Duple bodied Midland Red C1 under-floor engined coaches were built in 1948. When they were withdrawn from passenger service in the early 1960s, several were converted to dual-control driver-training vehicles and painted all-over red like this example in Herbert Road, Bearwood on a warm day in June 1969. Everyone wore their drivers' caps and the second steering wheel is clearly visible through the nearside windscreen. One of the survivors has been restored to its original condition, giving a reminder of how striking this design was when it first appeared, and what great ambassadors the vehicles were for the Midland Red company.
(Above, Malcolm Keeley; Right, John Senior)

fronted vehicles were ideal for this purpose, as trainer and trainee sat alongside each other and not only had they been converted to have two sets of pedals, but they also had two steering wheels as well. One could imagine the reaction of VOSA to such a vehicle today. The first lesson started with steering, and once I was doing this to Obe's satisfaction, I progressed to using the foot brake and then the accelerator. Midway through the second lesson we progressed to gear changing, the most important of the arts which had to be mastered in order to propel a bus built in the 1950s through your driving test. Successful double de-clutching to change crash box gears is all about timing and I shall never forget driving round the streets of Wolverhampton

shouting in unison with Obe "out together - 2 - 3 - in together". It was a technique that I found myself repeating, albeit silently, when I later drove D7 double-deckers in service. It worked so well, that apart from starting from rest, it was possible to dispense with the use of the clutch pedal altogether, making life considerably easier for the muscles in your left leg. While I had mastered the Midland Red gear box with some expertise, I later learnt that just as others had difficulty with the Midland Red gear change, I was to struggle with Leylands, AECs, Bristols and just about everything else with a crash gearbox.

The Transport and General Workers' Union full time officer representing Midland Red drivers and conductors for many years was

Midland Red's most-renowned double-decker was the 72-seat D9. This example, 4849, entered service in 1960 and was one of the vehicles transferred to West Midlands PTE in 1973. It is standing at the temporary Bull Ring terminus in Birmingham surrounded by new construction work. The young man queuing in the right foreground appears mesmerized by the vehicle – perhaps a budding bus enthusiast? (Roy Marshall)

Ken Coleclough. Ken had an advantage over the senior management sitting across the table from him, in that he was an ex-Midland Red driver from Stafford and consequently knew more about the Company that they ever did; he had also participated in Company pay negotiations for a number of years. I witnessed one particular platform staff pay negotiation which was revolutionary for its time. Like much of the industry, the Midland Red unions were utterly opposed to anyone other than drivers and conductors working on the road except in emergency and also to the use of part time staff. The then current thinking of both sides was, given the difficulties recruiting and retaining staff, that if the regular staff were to work Monday to Friday duties, the Saturday and Sunday work could become overtime if there was also an agreement enabling the use of part-time and other staffs to help cover weekend work. It was an enormous leap of faith to expect that the weekend work would be covered, but the agreement was that management and unions would work together locally to ensure the work was covered. The deal was all but done, when Ken Coleclough produced one final negotiating demand. The unions would only agree the deal if the drivers had basic pay parity across all 33 garages, which in effect meant significant pay rises at the smaller rural garages. Management got their calculators out and eventually conceded the request but with the gift of hindsight, this was a fundamental error which hastened the demise of the Company. Rural garages did not have the same recruitment issues as the urban ones and the pay rates awarded in Ludlow, for example, meant that the Midland Red drivers were earning almost as much as the town's bank manager!

The Monday to Friday working week experiment produced mixed results. Some garages managed to cover their weekend work well but others, particularly in the Birmingham and the Black Country really struggled. However, it was good news for me as a trainee as there was now plenty of opportunity to work on the road at weekends whenever I wanted to. I worked out of Bearwood as my "home" garage but I was also asked to go to Digbeth and Sheepcote Street at short notice to cover duties on services I didn't know. Route learning in those straightened times was a nicety which could be dispensed with, if the need arose.

I recall my first occasion working the 144 to Worcester and Malvern with my conductor periodically kneeling on the lower saloon offside front passenger seat giving me left and right hand signals on the way there and back. I had to view these signals through the internal mirror as it was Midland Red policy not to have a sliding communication window between the driver's cab and the saloon. A Saturday late duty on service 162 from Birmingham to Chelmsley Wood was more of a challenge as this service was one-person operated. I reported for duty and asked for a map, only to be told, "don't worry the passengers will tell you where to go". I started to load the vehicle in Birmingham Bus Station and asked a succession of boarding passengers if they could show me the route. My request was greeted with incredulity by some, who thought I was "having a laugh" but, when pressed, confessed they didn't pay much attention to the route as it ran limited stop for much of its length. Eventually an old man boarded who not only knew the way but was prepared to stand beside me for his journey and navigate for me. I thought it was the least I could do to give him a free ride but I was suspicious that he might take me to his front door and then leave me to work the rest out for myself!

D-Day, Monday 15th February 1971, the day the nation switched to decimal currency, was another memorable challenge. I somehow finished up conducting on a service I didn't know. It was no use asking the passengers what they had paid the last time they travelled as there was no way of relating this to the fares in the new currency. In truth they were just as confused as I was and I was conscious that I also had to keep the bus moving by supervising the platform and ringing the driver off promptly. Somehow, I got through the duty, but I later wondered what a plain clothes Inspector, conducting a similar exercise to the one I had been given by Walter Womar, would have made of my antics.

I also recall the pitfalls of services which were worked by more than one garage. The 125/126 services between Birmingham and Wolverhampton via the New Road were worked by Bearwood, Oldbury, Dudley and Wolverhampton garages which, on paper, made for the most efficient schedules and minimized light running. But when each of the garages was struggling to cover duties it could lead to disastrous results as each independently made the decision to "take a bus off the New Road, as the others will be operating". One fateful Saturday, my conductor and I were the first bus to appear for an hour, on what should have been a 15 minute service. Not a good way to nurture your passengers – or to retain your conductors, given the abuse mine received that day.

Staff shortages were most damaging amongst the platform staff, which Midland Red and others sought to address by accelerating their programmes for conversion to one person operation (OPO), as they could then afford to pay OPO drivers a 25% premium over crew driver rates. There were problems on the Engineering side as well, some of which stemmed from increasing difficulties with sourcing parts for the company's home grown products. I well remember being instructed by depot engineering staff when taking particular buses out of the garage not to "switch off" at

This Midland Red built 45-seat dual-purpose S22, is one of 37 delivered in 1968 for OPO long distance stage services. The black roof signifying dual-purpose status had by then been abandoned. In 1970, 5894 awaits departure on the long established service from Leicester to Bagworth via Kirby Muxloe. (Roy Marshall)

terminal points for fear that the vehicle might not restart.

One Saturday I was working a late turn on a Bearwood local service with an S17 single-decker where the outer terminal was beside a tower block in a bus lay-by on the crest of a hill. While the "keep it running" instruction was ringing in my ears, I also knew that there had been complaints from residents and a Traffic Instruction was on the Notice Board reminding drivers to switch off at that particular terminus. I weighed up my options and the Traffic Instruction won. The departure was around 7pm and the younger residents were coming out in their glad rags ready for a night on the town. Departure time came and surprise, surprise – the starter failed. My passengers were ready to party and would not have taken kindly to a long wait for a changeover to arrive, so I suggested that if they could push me off the top of the hill, I could drop it into gear as it gathered speed on the downward gradient and that would start the bus. About six young men and women bought into my proposal and pushed the bus sufficiently hard to get it rolling. Fifty metres down the slope I slipped it into gear and the engine burst into life. As I braked to bring the vehicle to rest I glanced in my mirror to see a posse of young ladies tottering unsteadily at speed towards me on their high heeled shoes. With thanks all round and a few dirty hands, we were on our way.

These anecdotes all paint a picture of a Company in chaos. Of course it was not and in each of my tales the passengers all reached their destinations one way or another. Furthermore, stories about duties where nothing untoward happened don't make interesting reading. It was however, a very testing time for the business where despite its best efforts, it really struggled to maintain all of its services reliably.

I was to witness two fares increase applications in my time at Midland Red. These Public Inquiries were held at the Offices of the West Midlands Traffic Commissioners in Broad Street, Birmingham. John Else was the Chairman of the West Midlands area and these sittings were held jointly with the East Midlands area, whose chairman was Charles Sheridan. Hearings were listed for two days as every local authority was able to object if they wished, and many did so. The company used to engage a Barrister from London, Edgar Faye, to present its case and James Isaac, the Traffic Manager was in the hot seat along with Norman Rolfe, the Accountant. Midland Red fares applications at that time followed a certain pattern. Many Local Authorities would submit an objection but not actually put in an appearance to make their case. In those cases the Officers were merely covering the Councillors backs so that they could at least tell their Committees and the public via the Press that they had objected – but to no avail; others were more astute. However, before the hearings got properly under way, the Commissioners had first to contend with Leslie Huckfield, MP, the Honourable Member for Nuneaton. As the sitting started, he would rise to request that the Commissioners should give him a hearing and that he be permitted to do it there and then as he had important Parliamentary business to attend to in Westminster later that day. Huckfield would seek an adjournment usually on the grounds that Parliament had just legislated, or was just about to legislate for some measure which would change the need for the Company's applications. Edgar Faye would then rise to make a case for an immediate determination and to explain the detrimental effect on bus services if the applications were to be delayed. The Commissioners would then withdraw to consider the arguments and return some ten minutes later to dismiss the MP's request, at which Huckfield would gather up his papers and flounce out.

There were only two ways that an objector could hope to win his case against a fares application before the Traffic Commissioners. The first was to demonstrate that the Company did not need the additional money it was seeking to raise. This was all but impossible without the assistance of a forensic accountant who was capable of analysing the accounting documents and projections that the Company had submitted in evidence. The second and more effective way of achieving a better outcome for the objecting Authority was to challenge the way the Company was seeking to generate the extra revenue it needed in their particular area. Two Authorities which were particularly good at this were Shrewsbury Borough Council and Upton upon Severn Rural District Council, the latter of which employed retired transport consultant Charles Dunbar to represent it.

After James Isaac and Norman Rolfe had given their evidence, and been cross-examined by the objectors, it was the objectors' opportunity and they would each in turn make their cases and then have to face cross-examination by Edgar Faye. In both

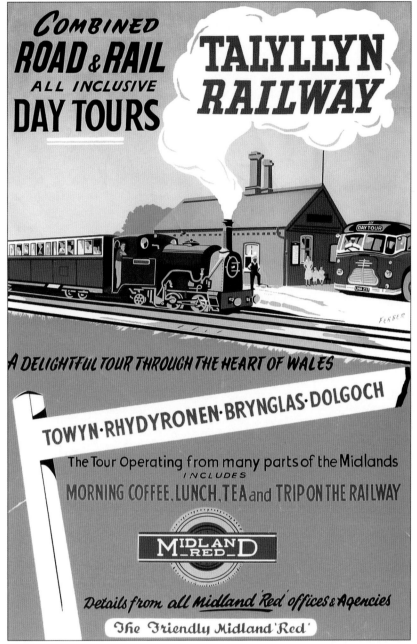

The regulation of fares was a cornerstone of the 1930 Transport Act and it went hand in hand with the route monopolies granted to operators by the Road Service Licensing system. However, by the 1970's when bus operators faced rapidly falling patronage and high cost inflation, the whole process was becoming over frequent and therefore ineffective, as later legislation was to recognise. At least the Commissioners were independent regulators who could call operators to account free from any local political influences. Their written decisions invariably contained insightful observations about the state of the bus industry and the measures that local authorities might take to promote the use of buses, rather than taking planning, highways and traffic management decisions which had precisely the opposite effect. The Commissioners did not pull any punches, as these remarks by John Else extracted from the written decision following the grant of the Midland Red July 1970 fares increase illustrate:

"The Commissioners are only too well aware that this decision, increasing the Midland Red fares by the largest amount authorised in its history – in fact more than twice as much as any previous grant – will not be received with acclamation by the objectors or the travelling public. It cannot be too widely known that the problems facing Midland Red in the West and East Midland Traffic Areas are not peculiar to that Company but are shared by all public transport undertakings throughout the country. In an industry in which over 2/3rds of the costs represent wages there is little hope of stabilising costs while present inflationary

the cases I witnessed, negotiations would take place between the parties at the end of the first day and they would inevitably be able to advise the Commissioners when the Public Inquiry reconvened that they had reached an agreement that in the case of their particular local authority areas the proposals should be agreed, but with modification. The Commissioners would retire at the end of the submissions by each of the objecting parties and the summing up by Edgar Faye and would usually return about half an hour later to grant the applications, as amended in the case of Shrewsbury and Upton upon Severn. A date for implementation would be confirmed and the Commissioners would later provide their written decision.

trends continue. It is said that higher fares, basically the result of higher wages, are the cause of passenger decline. At the best this is a half truth for there is ample evidence that the growth in the ownership and use of the private car (quadrupled over the last twenty and doubled in the last ten years) and changed social habits bear an equal if not greater responsibility. Irregularity and unreliability of services, whether caused by staff shortage or road congestion, are also serious factors in passenger decline."

The wisdom of these remarks remains just as relevant now, over 40 years later.

Company car policy was always a potentially divisive issue, and can still be today – something I always found odd in businesses devoted to providing public transport but, as in society at large, your company car defined your status in the eyes of your peers and those you knew "off the job". Midland Red tackled this by rigidly applying its car allocations to different grades of staff. The Ford Motor Company had long appreciated these issues which were common in status conscious corporate Britain and marketed a range of cars suited to any corporate pecking order. All Midland Red company cars were black Fords, with the exception of the General Manager's whose

chauffeur drove a black Jaguar. The Traffic Manager and Chief Engineer had Ford Consuls, the Divisional Traffic Managers and Engineers drove Ford Cortinas, as did the various Head Office heads of departments, and the Assistant Divisional Management were allocated Ford Escorts. Garage Engineers and Garage Traffic Superintendents, who wore glorified Inspectors' uniforms, were expected to ride buses or buy their own vehicles.

In those days, Midland Red had four Divisions, each with around 400 to 450 buses: Central covered garages in the Birmingham area together with Leamington, Lichfield and Tamworth, North West covered Staffordshire and Shropshire, South covered Worcestershire and Herefordshire and North East covered Leicestershire and Warwickshire garages. The Divisional management largely comprised career busmen who were in their 50s or early 60s, with one exception – the Traffic team at North East.

While the D9 was still in production, Midland Red purchased a batch of 50 Alexander-bodied Daimler CRG6LX DD11 front-entrance double-deckers in 1963. Further orders were placed for 150 dual-entrance DD12 vehicles to a similar specification in 1966 which were followed by the DD13s in 1969. This 74-seat example is seen arriving in Dudley on the Birmingham - Wolverhampton service 126 via the New Road with ruins of the castle prominent on the skyline. (Geoffrey Morant)

My Traffic training took me to Leicester for six weeks, where I was under the tutelage of North East Divisional Traffic Manger, Roger Dixon and his Assistant, Ken Newman. Roger was definitely not a product from the Midland Red mould. He was a lot younger than his peers and had spent time in the Royal Air Force. Roger and Ken worked from a Divisional Office in Peacock Lane, Leicester, beside the Southgate Street garage. Along with the Divisional Clerk, a man by the name of Richardson, who also had a Services background, they shared one office and sat round a large boardroom table with Dixon at the head and his two lieutenants on the sides. In those days before mobile telephones, the standard Post Office land line was the fastest way of communication and it was Richardson's job to field all incoming phone calls. Roger Dixon's philosophy was that work should be fun and between them they had worked out a signalling protocol for dealing with important internal telephone calls.

The system was as follows: if the Traffic Manager was on the phone, Richardson would cover the mouthpiece and announce in a serious tone "amber alert". If the Deputy General Manager was calling he would cover the mouthpiece and announce in a slightly more urgent tone "red alert". On the rare occasions that the General Manager should ring, the announcement in strident tones would be "triple brown alert", at which point all three would rise to their feet, stand to attention and salute. I doubt that any of these Birmingham bigwigs were aware of the irreverent way their incoming communications were being announced. Roger Dixon also bent Company rules by customizing his company Ford Cortina. Whilst nothing was visible externally, he had fitted twin-tone air horns under the bonnet, which were particularly popular with boy racers at that time. I was treated to a demonstration on one ride round rural Leicestershire – very impressive they were too.

Another character who stood out from the pack, but in a very different way, was Guy Baker. Guy's title was Liaison Officer and he was one of the General Manager's small reporting team. A bachelor in his fifties, Guy was a heavy cigarette smoker and used to carry a little marble egg in his pocket as his equivalent of the modern day stress buster. His father had been General Manager of Birmingham City Transport and Guy was a cultured man and something of a gourmet. He particularly liked classical music and he told me how he played his record player like a juke box. Each December he would select a new composer for the ensuing year and would buy himself for Christmas one recording of his chosen musician. Then each time he played it, he would place a shilling (5p) in a jar. Once he had sufficient in the jar to purchase another recording of the said composer, he would do so. And so the more he liked the composer's music, the more he played it and the more he played it, the more shillings he collected and the more shillings he collected, the more records he would buy.

Guy did those jobs which didn't fall to anyone else and this included dealing with the County Councils on major planning or highways applications which might affect the Company's operations. Whilst spending a few days with Guy he had arranged to meet the Traffic Superintendent in Hereford to discuss plans he had received for a new highways scheme in the town, which might disadvantage the bus services. I asked him the day before what time we would be leaving, expecting there to be an early start as Hereford was sixty miles away and before the days of motorways, this was likely to be a two hour journey. "Be ready to leave at 11.30am," he said. And so we did. Just under an hour later as we approached the Chateau Impney Hotel near Droitwich Spa, Guy said "I think we had better stop here for lunch. Do you know, they have the best hors d'oeuvres in the area?" It certainly was the best I had ever encountered and about an hour and a half later we were once more on our way.

Eventually, around 3.30 pm, we arrived in Hereford to be welcomed by the Traffic Superintendent who had all but given us up for lost. The next two hours were spent discussing the impact of the proposals and walking the affected area and by six o'clock we were back in Guy's black Cortina heading towards Birmingham. "I think we'll get a few miles under our belts before we stop for dinner", said Guy. As I recall, we made it back to Worcester where Guy announced he knew a nice little restaurant which would be ideal for our evening meal. Guy certainly knew how to time his journeys to ensure that the Company fed him well but I reasoned that Walter Womar must have been happy to tolerate his excesses since it was he who signed off Guy's expenses. Perhaps the fact that Guy was allowed to continue living high on the hog, when the Company was struggling for profitability, was just one more indicator that the Midland Red Company was reaching the end of an era.

THE LITTLE COMPANY WITH THE BIG HEART

My first post on completion of the National Bus Company senior management training scheme was in Yorkshire, with the Yorkshire Woollen District Transport Company Limited. However, before appointment I was required to attend a formal interview with the General Manager, Fred Dark. It would then be Fred's decision as to whether or not I would join his team. The interview was in the second week of my final training stint which was based at NBC's New Street Square head office in London. I rose early at my hotel on Southampton Row and set off for Kings Cross to catch the 7am train to Wakefield where I was to be met by Fred's chauffeur. The journey north was spent thinking about the questions I might be asked and preparing appropriate answers to them when, an hour into the journey, I looked down and noticed that I had managed to put on odd socks.

Sugar! What was I to do? We were already rattling towards Wakefield where the chauffeur was to meet me. I decided that my only salvation was to find a pair of socks before I got there. I set off down the train more in hope than expectation, until eventually I spied a naval rating asleep in one compartment, with a potentially vital suitcase in the rack above his head. I entered the compartment and woke the slumbering sailor with an "Excuse me, mate"

uttered at a volume which would wake but not alarm him. I explained my predicament and asked him if I might buy a pair of his socks. He took his case from the rack and asked me what colour I was looking for, to which I replied "anything dark – so long as they match". Out came a pair of well-worn dark grey socks and I offered him a fiver for his trouble. Suitably matched, I stepped off the train in Wakefield to be met by the chauffeur who escorted me to Fred's office. Some twelve months later I told Fred the story, to which he responded, "You needn't have bothered; if I had noticed I would have thought that it was the latest in trendy London fashion".

NBC was barely three years old and Yorkshire Woollen had just been merged with the neighbouring West Riding Road Car Company based in Wakefield. Fred Dark and his management team had recently moved over to the bigger Head Office at Belle Isle and I had been appointed Assistant Traffic

Yorkshire Woollen District operated a mixed fleet, typified by this 1972 scene at Dewsbury Bus Station. The ungainly looking double-decker was originally a Leyland Tiger PS2/5 saloon, re-bodied by Roe with 63 seats in 1963. It is following a very smoky Leyland Leopard, just out of camera. The service 57 bus is an Alexander-bodied Daimler CRG6LX behind which are two 53-seat Willowbrook bodied Leyland PSU3/1s.
(Geoffrey Morant)

Superintendent at Dewsbury, the old Woollen head office, to learn the ropes from Traffic Superintendent Eric Pollard, who was just a year off retirement. Aside from this, my role was to aid the integration of the Woollen and West Riding Companies.

Yorkshire Woollen felt like a family business. When I arrived in 1971 there were only two depots – Saville Town in Dewsbury, beside the river Calder, and Beck Lane in Heckmondwike, just 3 miles away. The company was proud of its history, which began in 1903, when the Yorkshire Woollen District Electric Tramways Limited started operations. The company's then owners, the British Electric Traction Company had agreed between 1898 and 1901 with eight local authorities to construct a 22 mile electric tramway system connecting the woollen district towns. When I arrived the company was providing an intense network of services between these towns and linking them with Halifax, Bradford, Leeds and Huddersfield – each of which had their own municipal bus operations. The financial obligations entered into under the 19th century tramway agreements remained in place and Dewsbury and Batley Councils were entitled to a profit share on certain of the bus routes, which had to

be accounted for separately. This had been their price for replacing the trams with motorbuses in 1934. I well recall being summoned to my first meeting with Batley Council to explain some proposed service revisions which we intended to make within the Borough. I went armed with passenger survey data, maps and timetables, well prepared for a rough ride from the Councillors. The meeting got underway and eventually we got to the bus services item. I did my best to explain the changes, the many benefits which would accrue to most passengers and the alternatives available to the unfortunate few who would lose out. Timetables and maps were handed round and I paused for questions. After what seemed to be an eternity, the Chairman piped up "Reet lad, we've heard all about t'changes, now tell us what they will do t'bus profits?" It was the one question I hadn't anticipated and I don't recall my reply, but it was sufficient for the Chairman to say "Next business".

Yorkshire Woollen staff were a long-serving and loyal group of employees, who were unimpressed that they were being merged with their rival in Wakefield although it helped that their own management team was still running the show, albeit from Belle Isle. I well remember a fares increase implementation, where Eric Pollard took me to a meeting with his West Riding counterparts to discuss the fares to be charged on common sections of route on the Wakefield-Morley-Bradford corridor. In those days of fares control by the Traffic Commissioners, it was common for one operator to set the fares on a given section of route and

Catching the 1971 morning sun en route to Dewsbury is this ex-Sheffield Joint Omnibus Committee 76-seat Metro-Cammell-bodied Leyland Atlantean PDR1/1. Service 4 was jointly operated with Bradford Corporation. It was not unusual for Bradford's Asian crews wishing to relocate to Dewsbury to enquire about job vacancies with YWD during their layover in Dewsbury bus station. (Geoffrey Morant)

for the others to "come into line". However, Eric had for many years conducted these fares negotiations in his own inimitable way which involved preparing two sets of fares charts – one for Yorkshire Woollen and a slightly higher one for the negotiations. As at that time, Inspectors from the two companies still only ever checked their own buses, Eric was able to ensure that Woollen buses were always a penny or two cheaper between the key fares stages. As we left the meeting I gently reminded Eric that we were now part of the same Group as West Riding to be firmly told "Yes, I know, but Yorkshire Woollen always comes first and the Group must come second". It was then that I realized, what the "aiding group integration" part of my job description was about.

The Woollen traffic office was home to some interesting characters, which would have provided enough material for a TV sitcom. Barbara Ryan, the Traffic Manager's secretary, who had been left behind when the senior management transferred to Wakefield was a thespian and not averse to displaying her amateur dramatic talents in the office, if things weren't going her way. On one occasion I was conducting drivers' trade union negotiations in my office, when the door nearly flew off its hinges as Barbara made a dramatic entrance. "Barbara", I said, "We are in a meeting" to which she replied. "I know, but this is important. Lionel Tuke, (the Insurance Officer), has just called me a third-rate prima donna, and I will not stand for it".

The schedulers were Ted, a Pole who had escaped to Britain during the war and never returned, instead settling in Yorkshire, and Albert Lockwood, a diehard old Yorkshireman who had never set foot outside the county. It was Albert who confirmed for me that the southerner's misconceptions about the geography of the north are matched by the northerner's misconceptions about the geography of the south. On first meeting Albert he asked where I was from to which I replied "Portsmouth". A little later in the conversation he enquired what it was like in Plymouth. I gently reminded him that I came from Portsmouth and knew little of Plymouth, to which he said "but they are next door to each other, aren't they?" I then had to tell him that it was nearly as far from Portsmouth to Plymouth as it was from Leeds to London only to be greeted with an incredulous, "Nay, lad".

Chief Inspector Fred Bradley was sometimes guilty of using excess initiative. I recall the morning after the tragic IRA coach bombing on the M62, when I nearly fell headlong over a bucket of sand on entering my office. Subsequent enquiries revealed that Fred

This 59-seat Roe-bodied Leyland PD2/30, originally new to the Sheffield Joint Omnibus Committee, is seen in Dewsbury bus station before departure on the Chickenley circular in April 1971. Its radiator grille is the familiar Midland Red design created for their Leyland LD8 vehicles. Yorkshire Woollen was a member of the busy Tyne-Tees-Mersey express coach service pool which is being promoted on the side of this vehicle. The two ladies are walking unchallenged across the bus station long before the days of risk assessments and hi-vis vests. (Roy Marshall)

had placed it there "just in case". My star in the Traffic Office however, was Richard Mitchell. Richard was responsible for traffic administration and was the first responder to telephone complaints. Everything about Richard was well ordered and every item on his desk was neatly set out, as if it had been placed there to the nearest millimetre. Richard had a way of dealing with complainants that meant they often finished their calls by apologizing to him for wasting his time. He had his own fan club and some callers used to ask for him by name. Indeed Fred Dark was in the Traffic Office one day, when Richard had left the room and his phone rang. Fred picked it up and the caller enquired to whom she was speaking. Fred replied, "My name's Dark, I'm General Manager". The caller responded curtly, "I don't want to speak to you. I want to speak to Mr Mitchell".

Fred was an inspirational General Manager whose exceptional man-management skills were all self-taught. He started his career as a Traffic Clerk at the Bristol Omnibus Company where according to Ken Hannis, a contemporary of his in those early days, Fred held the record for the quickest circumnavigation of the Bristol Company's very large Traffic Office. The rules apparently required that contestants had to touch all four walls without once touching the floor on their way round. This therefore necessitated leaping between various items of office furniture. Unfortunately, I did not learn

of this remarkable achievement until after Fred's death and was therefore unable to check its authenticity. Fred didn't hold with higher or further education and he once remarked to me that "management is like B.O. – you've either got it, or you ain't." Like many senior managers of his day, Fred was able to consume large amounts of alcohol without any apparent ill effects. We all dreaded the call at five o'clock, when Fred invited you to go down to his office. The working day was formally finished and the drinks cabinet was unlocked but if you got the call you knew you would be staying there for two or three hours while you and Fred put the company and the world to rights. I recall his wife taking me to one side at a function and warning me that despite his apparent inebriation, Fred would remember everything that was said by the next morning when he would be bright eyed and bushy-tailed just raring to go at 8.30am – while the rest of us were still struggling to find the keys let alone engage first gear.

Fred was always supportive of his management, particularly if the trades unions thought they might be able to go over our heads when the opportunity arose. At one Yorkshire

Approaching Huddersfield on the A62 in 1972, is one of a 1963 batch of 14 YWD Albion LR7 Lowlanders with Weymann 72-seat bodies. The two YWD direct services (18 & 19) from Leeds were never busy outside peak hours as this light loading testifies. (Geoffrey Morant)

New in 1976, this 73-seat Roe bodied, (built from Park Royal parts), Leyland Atlantean AN68/1R, is entering Huddersfield on one-man service 219 from Leeds later the same year. The 19 service number now has a 2 prefix and the livery is standard NBC poppy red, with NBC style Yorkshire logo. It has been released for service with a part-painted accident repair, suggesting that YWD engineers were struggling to meet service. In 1987 the West Riding Group management team bought the Group and this bus was reallocated to the newly created Sheffield and District operation. (Geoffrey Morant)

Woollen long service awards evening I noted that they had encircled Fred in a corner and were earnestly lobbying him. I guessed what it was about as I had just implemented a reschedule of the Birstall-Thornhill services, which, with Ted and Albert's assistance, had maintained the frequencies but saved a bus. Fred beckoned me over. On joining the party he said to me "They tell me that you have just taken a bus out of the Birstall-Thornhill services. How long have you given them from end to end?" I told him the new running time, I think it was 39 minutes. "39 minutes", said Fred, "I could do it on my d*** in half the time", at which the assembled gathering fell about laughing – and when they eventually composed themselves, Fred had slipped away.

Fred also stood up for the Company with NBC Headquarters when the need arose. Despite its small size and operating territory Yorkshire Woollen was the one Company that had claimed for itself the "Yorkshire" fleet name. West Riding Automobile Services, West Yorkshire Road Car Company, Yorkshire Traction Company and East Yorkshire Motor Services were bigger businesses, but it was Yorkshire Woollen that proudly displayed just the name Yorkshire. With Freddie Wood's arrival as NBC chairman in January 1972 came the decision to "go corporate" in a big way. That meant only three identical bus liveries red, green or blue throughout England and Wales, and the birth of National Express as the identity for the express coach service network. While the creation of a national brand for the coach network made excellent business sense, and it has survived largely unchanged to this day, the loss of local identities was much mourned in many companies.

At Yorkshire Woollen insult was added to injury when the instruction from New Street Square was that the fleet name would be changing to "Yorkshire WD". The staff were incensed and all credit went to Fred Dark for ensuring a speedy retraction. Yorkshire Woollen could keep its "Yorkshire" fleet name but lost its livery along with every other NBC subsidiary. Some staff were heard to mutter that perhaps it was no coincidence that the entire NBC fleet was going through a repaint so soon after Freddie Wood had arrived from Croda Paints! A nice theory but corporate branding was by then rampant throughout 1970s business and the conventional boardroom wisdom was that big really was beautiful – the complete antithesis of everything that Yorkshire Woollen had stood for.

The NBC logo first appeared in 1972. Norman Wilson, the industrial designer used by Croda Paints, was brought in by NBC Chairman, Sir Frederick Wood (himself ex-Croda) to produce this italicized N and its mirror image. For its day, it was dramatic. It was applied rigorously to buses, express coaches (which were painted all over white and branded NATIONAL EXPRESS), uniforms, stationery and premises signage. It conveyed movement and, when displayed in colour, a touch of quality. However, by modern design standards it might be seen as too geometric and devoid of any emotion. (National Bus Company, courtesy Kithead Trust)

TALES FROM THE WEST RIDING

Yorkshire Woollen's next door neighbour to the east was West Riding Automobile Services Limited. The characters of the two Companies were very different. Yorkshire Woollen principally served the mill towns of Yorkshire's heavy woollen district, whereas West Riding served the northern end of the Yorkshire coalfield and the county town of Wakefield. Furthermore, Woollen was a BET Company whereas Riding, along with Barton Transport and Lancashire United was one of the three remaining large independent Companies until its sale to the nationalized Transport Holding Company in 1967. West Riding was also about twice the size of Yorkshire Woollen.

The West Riding Company was born as the Yorkshire (West Riding) Electric Tramways Company Limited in 1904. The trams last ran in 1932 but bus services had started on Easter Monday 1922. The West Riding company was formed in 1923 as a subsidiary to operate the motor bus side of the business. The Company doubled in size with the acquisition of Bullocks of Featherstone in 1950 and at the time of its nationalization was running some 400 buses.

In the 1960s West Riding was noted for its unusual bus fleet. It had jointly developed with Guy Motors of Wolverhampton the Guy Wulfrunian, a front-engined, front-entrance double-decker with Charles Roe bodies from nearby Leeds. These vehicles made up over 30% of its fleet. The Wulfrunian was launched at the Commercial Motor Show in 1958 as a concept double-deck vehicle for one-person operation and was the first double-deck service bus to offer air suspension and disc brakes.

In total 137 Wulfrunians were built, with 126 going to West Riding. Guy had pinned its hopes on the vehicle becoming a winner for them but, unfortunately, the suspension and braking systems proved unreliable and costly to maintain. Guy produced demonstrators but there were few sales elsewhere. The few that were sold failed to generate any further orders and six more of the total production eventually came second-hand to West Riding. West Riding

While Leyland, Bristol and Daimler were developing rear-engined chassis suitable for one-person double-deck operation, Guy came up with the idea of a front entrance, front-engined bus, with the driver squeezed alongside the engine. It wasn't a success. Here, 75-seat Roe bodied Guy Wulfrunian 909 arrives in Leeds Central Bus Station in 1969. (John May)

had ordered a further 25 Wulfrunians, but given
the apparently insoluble reliability problems,
then cancelled them. For Guy Motors it was the
gamble that failed. The Wulfrunian development
costs and lack of orders to recover them brought
an end to bus production in 1964 and was a
major contributor to the manufacturer's demise
as an independent. Guy became part of the
British Leyland empire in 1968.

One of the National Bus Company's early
decisions, apart from the merger of the Woollen
and West Riding Companies, was the drafting
in of buses to accelerate the replacement of the
Wulfrunians and the Company was fortunate
that there were significant numbers of much
more reliable double- deckers becoming surplus
to requirements in sister companies as a result
of the drive towards one-person double-deck
operation.

I can recall that even within West Riding
there were differences of culture, with the ethos
at the Selby depot more akin to that which I
knew at Yorkshire Woollen. I remember one
Traffic Management meeting held at the Belle
Isle head office in 1972, when we reported on
our response to a rail strike which had occurred
the week before. At Woollen we had duplicated
our peak hour Dewsbury services into Leeds,
which had been loaded to the gunnels. At the
central West Riding depots the drivers' trade
union had refused to man any extra services,
as they regarded it to be strike breaking,
but at Selby, George Beal the local Traffic
Superintendent had, for the duration of the
strike, quietly run a couple of peak duplicates

By the time NBC had acquired West Riding, Wulfrunian
reliability problems were seriously affecting services, and
vehicles like this Bristol LD6G were drafted in from other
Group companies. This particular example, with 70-seat ECW
bodywork, leaving Wakefield Bus Station in October 1969 came
from Midland General. (Geoffrey Morant)

into and out of York, which had done very
nicely, thank you.

Mark Fowles arrived at West Riding as an
NBC senior management trainee in 1984. He
recalls his early experiences under the watchful
eye of the company's Training Manager, Anton
Michelle. Mark was initially assigned to the
Belle Isle Depot where he was to learn the
ropes as a conductor and found that the District
Manager exhibited a particular hostility to
management trainees. Most employees would
take trainees as they found them but there
were a few who resented young men (and they
were all men in those days) who were full of
bright ideas and countless questions. Some had
had a bad experience with a previous trainee
and therefore assumed that you would be no
different. A few genuinely resented the fact that
the training scheme was producing individuals
who would block their own routes to promotion.
These were all challenges for each individual
trainee to overcome by gaining the confidence of
each of his mentors.

In this case however, Mark sensed that
Charlie's (as we will call him) resentment
ran deep and was therefore not surprised
when he was scheduled to work the earliest
of early duties and the latest of lates on the
toughest services, including the last Portobello

Also drafted in to West Riding was this 74-seat Northern Counties-bodied Dennis Loline III, a chassis built under licence from Bristol Commercial Vehicles. New in 1967, it was one of five similar buses purchased from the Halifax Joint Omnibus Committee. Seen leaving Wakefield for Ossett, the border town with neighbouring Yorkshire Woollen District, it carries National Bus Company advertisements proclaiming West Riding's new corporate affiliation. (John May)

on Christmas Eve. He describes the duty as follows.

"Now the day had gone well really without too many issues. We had trundled up and down between Lupset and Portobello and whilst I had to contend with a passenger vomiting, this was soon dealt with by opening the windows and a quick mop out as we passed through the bus station midway through the journey. The real problem came on the last trip of the evening with a full load of merry (and not so merry) tough northern males playing to the gallery of their equally merry women folk. Collecting fares on the lower deck was a breeze; everyone was singing and having a laugh and a joke. As we travelled along Barnsley Road I made my way up the stairs and as my head just appeared above floor level I looked to the rear of the bus to be greeted by a shout from the largest Neanderthal male you could have the misfortune to meet. It went something like, 'You're not getting a f****** thing off me – I've spent it all on booze'. He then began laughing, egged on by his mates who provided verbal and moral support.

"I moved to the front of the bus and started to collect the fares and as I made my way down the bus the Neanderthal was bellowing all

the time, 'You're not getting a f******penny from me!' Not wishing to antagonize the man, who by this point was blocking all the light out, I decided to engage in some light banter and replied, 'You can have this one on me. It's Christmas after all'. It was only when I was behind him leaning against a pole, steadying myself that things began to go wrong.

"Just as we started to turn from Barnsley Road into Portobello Road, Arnie, my driver, slammed on the brakes in order to avoid a car coming off the dual carriageway. Now, we weren't going that fast but it was enough to knock me off balance and throw me up the aisle and onto the floor I distinctly remember just as I was flying through the air, feeling my neck being yanked by something and hearing a simultaneous Aaaah 'F***!' As I hit the floor, most of the change in my bag spilled out and I busied myself with getting it together. As I turned around to get up, the Neanderthal was standing over me holding the back of his head, from which there was blood flowing. He was extending his other hand towards me with some loose change in it and staring me straight in the eye said, 'Here's your f****** fare, no need for that' and then sat down, quiet as a mouse.

"Judging by the state of the outer case of my Almex ticket machine, with its crack and blood stains, the 'yank' as I'd flown though the air must have been the machine colliding with his head. As we approached the terminus he still hadn't alighted and being the brave, practical minded person I was, I hid in the luggage area below the stairs pulling the canvas curtain

In 1967 West Riding purchased a batch of ten 51-seat Roe bodied Leyland PSUR1/1s. This immaculately turned out example is seen a year later. However, to add to the Company's woes, the rear-engined Panther was as mechanically unreliable as the Wulfrunian. (Geoffrey Morant)

across until he'd got off and we were on our way back to depot. Thankfully it was my last duty ever on that service."

At this time, the West Yorkshire Passenger Transport Authority was the Metropolitan County Council and Mark observed that Charlie's contempt for senior management trainees was matched by his contempt for county councillors. One particular councillor, who represented a small village in the south of our operating area, was also a member of the council's Transport Committee and had made it his personal goal to have a bus station built in this village. For what purpose Mark couldn't understand, as the village only had one or two services an hour and a more than adequate turnaround for buses smack bang in the middle of the village. This is how Mark says the story unfolded.

"For several years the councillor lobbied for funds to create his bus station and having secured the money spent a few more years trying to locate a suitable site for the facility. However, every time he came up with a site Charlie provided a "genuine" reason as to why it was not suitable. Finally, a plot of land came on to the market which was located to the rear of some shops facing the existing bus turnaround. The councillor asked our intrepid District

Manager to consider it. Once again Charlie came up with an excuse, "The gap is too narrow between the shops for the buses to get in and out of " he replied. The councillor was not to be deflected so arrangements were made for us to try and take a bus through the gap with both the councillor and officials from the Transport Authority in attendance.

"Charlie took me along to the trials. As we boarded the bus before leaving Belle Isle, Charlie had a word with the driver along the lines of "I don't care what you have to do but if you get this bus through that gap without hitting something I'll f****** thump you". With those words ringing in the driver's ears, we set off for the trial. Now, unsurprisingly, the driver managed not only to scrape the near side as he squeezed through the gap, but he also hit the front off side at the same time. It was a masterly piece of driving by anyone's standards. The second attempt proved no more successful and resulted in a cracked front screen. All present concluded that the gap was

West Riding's predecessor, the Wakefield & District Light Railway Company, began tramway operations in August 1904. This 1969 76-seat Roe bodied Daimler CRG6LX was re-painted in 1984 to mark the 80th anniversary. (Geoffrey Morant)

far too narrow even though I, as a mere novice PSV driver, could have taken a bus through this gap blindfolded and still with room to spare. Once again the councillor would have to shelve his latest plans. On the journey back to Belle Isle, Charlie congratulated the driver on a masterly exhibition of appalling driving and that was that or so we thought . . .

"About a year passed and once again the issue of the bus station for the village was raised. Again, we were asked to take a bus along to try out the new site. This time it wasn't a new site but the old one with the same point of access. However, now there was a shop missing! It had been demolished and the gap was now so wide that even a blind man could have driven through it without touching either side.

It transpired that the councillor wasn't going to be defeated by a mere access problem and following our abortive trials he had gone away and through a compulsory purchase order process had acquired one of the adjoining

premises enabling them to be demolished. An "appropriate" access and egress was thus created and the bus station was duly constructed. It still stands to this day, in my opinion as a monument to the folly of pride in local politics."

By the time Mark had been at West Riding for nearly two years the integration of the Yorkshire Woollen and West Riding Companies had been in place for over 13 years. However, Mark was still able to detect the differences in staff attitude between the two constituent parts of the Group when he was sent to Heckmondwike as relief Depot Manager. I will let Mark tell the story.

"This is a tale of young innocence. Being very keen at that time to make an impression, one of the first tasks I undertook was to review all those employees on long term sick leave. Having been through the process several times I was getting quite used to the interview routine and subsequent discussion with the trade union and the individual concerned, who it has to be said mostly, had genuine conditions. However, I stumbled on one particular case concerning a gentleman, whom I'll call Mr Smith to spare his blushes. I was convinced I'd found someone swinging the lead as his sick notes indicated that he was off with "flatulence" and had been so for over six months.

"Well this all appeared a bit odd to a young naïve manager. Why had no one else picked up on this previously? A letter was soon dispatched to Mr Smith requesting his attendance at an interview the following week. On the day of the interview there was a knock on the door and in walked Fred Sharpe, the TGWU union rep, accompanied by said Mr Smith. Usually after entering Fred would shut the door and we then get down to business but on this occasion he left the door open. I got up and closed the door and having done so turned to go back to my desk. It was at that point that I noticed Fred was opening a window, which was strange considering the cool and wet weather conditions. I really should have twigged at that point but didn't, even when Fred moved his seat back a considerable distance from Mr Smith, I

was still totally unprepared for what was about to happen.

"It was only when I asked after Mr Smith's well-being that a large paaaaaarp! came from behind him followed by the most obnoxious odour you have ever smelt in your life, that I began to realise that our Mr Smith had a very genuine complaint. After a short adjournment, I decided to conclude the interview in the car park, where I was to learn that the previous manager had taken Mr Smith off duties following numerous complaints from passengers. It transpired that Mr Smith had a VERY nervous stomach. Whenever a passenger or anyone else, including me, asked him a question there followed a paaaaaarp, which was accompanied by that terrible smell. He never did come back to work and whenever I saw Fred subsequently we would both fall about laughing at each retelling of this tale."

This brace of Guy Wulfrunians with 75-seat bodies by Charles Roe of Leeds and seen below, date from 1960. West Riding then applied both red and green liveries, the red vehicles being deployed on the ex-tram routes. All but eleven Wulfrunians were purchased new by West Riding. Two were bought by Accrington Corporation and specified with open rear platform East Lancs bodywork, seemingly combining all of the challenges of the Wulfrunian with none of its potential benefits! (Below: Alan Montgomery; Right: John Senior)

EXPRESS SERVICES

Before 1970 the majority of express services were provided by the Tilling and BET Companies although some were provided by famous independent companies like Barton, Yclloway and Premier Travel. Express services were big business in their heyday and in the 1960s carried over 75 million passengers a year. Even in 1975 they accounted for 10% of NBC company mileage which by then operated 82% of the nation's express coach services using the National Express (NE) brand.

Until 1980, express services were regulated by the road service licensing system which had been created by the 1930 Road Traffic Act. To introduce or amend a licensed express service the operator was required to submit an application to the Traffic Commissioners in the area where the service originated with backing applications for each other traffic area through which it passed. Objections could be lodged by other operators, local authorities on line of route, the Police and British Rail. If the objections were not withdrawn then a Public Inquiry would be held at which the Commissioners would determine whether or not the application was in the public interest. Making the case for new express services was not easy, as those operators already licensed for particular destinations would argue that new services would abstract their passengers and put their own services at risk.

Perhaps because of these licensing hurdles many services were jointly provided by a number of operators through pooling agreements which entitled the parties to an agreed percentage of the revenue and the mileage operated. The largest pool operated under the Associated Motorways banner. Created in 1934, it operated a hub-and-spoke model through Cheltenham, which became a major interchange for services from the Midlands & North West, London & the South East and the South West & Wales. Its operating members were Black & White, Red & White, Midland Red, Bristol Greyhound and Royal Blue, which was the coaching arm of Southern and Western National. After the war Crosville, Lincolnshire Road Car, Eastern Counties and later Southdown joined the pool. At the height of the season, Associated Motorways offered up to 800 journeys per day. Other pools provided the Tyne-Tees-Mersey, London-Scotland, and the Newcastle-Birmingham (Ten Cities)

This mid-50s scene at Victoria Coach Station includes a typical array of contemporary coaches. From left to right are a 1954 Midland Red C3 with 37-seat Willowbrook bodywork, two 1953 Southdown 41-seat Duple bodied Leyland PSU1/16s, an indeterminate ECW bodied Bristol LS, a trio of Maidstone & District 37-seat Harrington bodied AEC Reliances, another indeterminate vehicle and a pair of East Kent 41-seat Duple bodied Dennis Lancets. The line up is completed by an ECW-bodied Bristol LS bound for the West Country. (Kithead Trust)

This Black & White 47-seat Plaxton Panorama bodied Leyland Leopard pauses in Gloucester in 1970 en route to Cheltenham to interchange with other Associated Motorways services. (Roy Marshall)

services. The Manchester-Birmingham-London corridor was one of the larger pools in which Ribble, North Western and Midland Red each had an interest.

Negotiations between the parties over the timetables and allocation of car workings tended to take place in the "close season" and I recall Derek Fytche, as Traffic Manager, attending one such negotiation on behalf of the North Western Company. Returning from the meeting he wrote to his counterpart at Midland Red to confirm his proposals. Within days he was himself promoted to the Midland Red Traffic Manager's post, enabling him to write back to North Western rejecting their (and his own) proposals.

In the 1950s and 60s summer seasonal express services took thousands of working folk and their families to the coast for their annual holiday fortnights. At these times towns and cities would decamp to their nearest seaside resort. Birmingham would descend on Weston-super-Mare or the North Wales coast, Leicester would head for Skegness and Mablethorpe, while Manchester favoured Blackpool. I recall being detailed at Midland Red Leicester at 5am one Saturday morning in 1970 to help clear Southgate Street depot of service buses. These were parked in surrounding streets

for their crews to collect, so that the depot could be used as a coach station for every coach and dual-purpose vehicle the division possessed, to transport what seemed to be the entire population of Leicester to the East Coast. Peak movements of this nature were commonplace and the impact on local bus services by the diversion of both buses and drivers from stage carriage to coastal services was often significant, although no one seemed to complain, perhaps because there were so few people left to do so.

One Friday night, four years later, I was in the Newcastle Civic Centre banqueting suite to mark the retirement of United's Northumberland Area Traffic Superintendent, Havelock Farrer, when we were approached by an ashen faced Tony Kennan. He had just been notified by staff at Gallowgate Coach Station that they had discovered 400 uncharted tickets on the chartroom window sill for the following morning's Newcastle-London express service. Fortunately there were representatives of almost every north-east bus and coach operator present and between us we somehow managed in the course of the evening, to find him eight 49 and 53-seat coaches and drivers to duplicate his service. This was no mean feat on the eve of a peak summer Saturday, particularly as it was accomplished without the aid of mobile phones.

London was the most important destination for many express coach journeys, the majority of which terminated at Victoria Coach Station. Originally opened in 1932 by London Coastal

Cheltenham Coach Station, the primary Associated Motorways interchange, was the home base of Black & White Motorways (BW). the coach operator jointly owned by Midland Red, Bristol and City of Oxford. This May 1967 scene captures a quieter moment as further arrivals are awaited. The BW coach bound for Bristol, a 1964 41-seat Harrington Cavalier AEC Reliance, is flanked by a Lichfield-bound Midland Red 49 dual-purpose seated S21, only a few weeks old, and a 37-seat C5 advertising the perils of nationalization. (Ray Stenning)

Coaches, it is now managed by Transport for London and serves 1200 UK and 400 European destinations. At its busiest during the holiday seasons, it would also experience very high demand during rail strikes. David Humphrey relates one such occasion in the early 1980s.

"In 1982 there was a two-week national rail strike. The National Express network immediately came under enormous pressure as rail passengers sought alternative means of travel. Victoria Coach Station tried to take the place of the eleven main line railway termini. The call went out to all the NBC subsidiaries to send staff to Victoria for the duration, to assist in the booking office and supervision of the station. At Bristol we sent several people up to help. After it was over, I asked one of the Inspectors how it went.

" He told me how, when he had got off the coach, they had put a clipboard in his hand with a plan of the bus station and all the departure bays and told him to 'stand over there and answer questions'." He had been getting on fine, directing people to Barnsley and all sorts of places he had never heard of, when his brain became completely stuck as someone asked him, "where can I buy an ice cream?" Before he

could get his brain back into gear, a vicar came up to him and asked how to get to Canterbury. Without even thinking he had told him, "the best bet for you right now is to get promoted".

Before the days of motorways the term express service was something of a misnomer. The South Coast Express journey between Margate and Bournemouth, which was jointly operated by East Kent, Southdown and Royal Blue, took eleven and three quarter hours to complete. Midland Red's Birmingham-Llandudno service took a scheduled six hours, and its Birmingham-London service was a five hour twenty minute journey. The opening of the motorways brought new opportunities to cut journey times, however, and Midland Red was one of the first to seize the opportunity, with new coaches specifically designed to run at motorway speeds.

In anticipation of the opening of the MI motorway in November 1959, General Manager, Donald Sinclair called in his Development Engineer, Jim Pearson and told him to produce a motorway coach capable of sustained 80 miles per hour cruising, it having been confirmed that there would be no speed limits on the motorway, then under construction. To add to the challenge, there was to be fleet of ten vehicles available for the day of the official opening. Pearson and his team took a Midland Red C5 coach off the production line and started to work out how they would increase the C5's maximum speed of 48 miles per hour by 75%. They calculated that they need a power output of 130 bhp, rather than the C5's standard 98 bhp and opted for a BSA turbocharger, a BMMO specified David Brown 5-speed gearbox and a Kirkstall 4.44:1 rear axle. Then it was off to MIRA for testing in March 1959. Mechanically the modified coach performed excellently and was very steady at high speed, but various other problems manifested themselves. Windscreen wipers needed stronger springs if they were to remain on the screen and high pressure windscreen washers were needed, as at 85 mph the washer fluid was going straight over the roof. Production could then begin, and the CM5Ts seated 34 passengers against the C5's 37 because of the provision of a toilet compartment.

In October 1958 applications for an express carriage road service licence for the Birmingham-London motorway service were submitted to the Traffic Commissioner, which attracted the inevitable objection from British Rail. After a Public Inquiry the application was granted in April 1959 but departures were restricted to three a day in each direction, with a maximum of two duplicates on each, with only one on the 6.30pm departure from London.

On 2nd November 1959 two coaches left Digbeth coach station in Birmingham for the round trip to London at around 8.30am. The first carried Donald Sinclair and VIPs with the second carrying the media including a BBC TV crew. Pearson and his team were not yet satisfied that they had the right tyres for high speed coach operation and a ghost coach followed discreetly behind with a set of spare wheels in the boot. His foresight was justified as on the return trip the VIP coach blew its nearside front tyre on the approach to the M45. The wheel change was quickly completed and Donald Sinclair was able to tell the assembled media at Digbeth that they had still arrived in Birmingham on schedule. No fewer than 15 different tyre specifications were tried before they could settle on one entirely suited to high-speed coach operation.

Midland Red was not the only express service operator to make use of the M1 on its first day of opening. Standerwick, Ribble's coaching subsidiary, also ran its prototype coach-seated Gay Hostess Leyland Atlantean that day and the Ribble crew talked of being overtaken by the Midland Red party. At that time the Atlanteans were only capable of 48 miles per hour. There was a story circulating in the North West that on their return journeys from London the Midland Red coaches again overtook the Gay Hostess, only to be re-overtaken following the blow-out incident. While this is good tortoise and hare material, the Midland Red

wheel changeover was undertaken so quickly that the alleged Standerwick victory may well be wishful thinking.

Operating experience showed that the initial journey time of 3 hours 25 minutes was excessive and it was progressively reduced to 2 hours 55 minutes and then to 2 hours 25 minutes. The national media coverage of the service and the attractive 21/3d return fare, (£1.06), ensured demand was high and Midland Red was soon applying to the Traffic Commissioner arguing for more duplication to be permitted. As a result, in 1961 the maximum number of duplicates permitted was increased to six on every departure.

I often drove south on the M1 on a Friday night in 1970 and was able to observe the northbound coaches on the 6.30pm departure from Victoria as they rushed north. Despite the railways attempt to limit passenger abstraction by restricting the number of licensed timetable departures, it became common knowledge that duplicates would leave as soon as they were full. So in practice, the first coach to leave Victoria on the 6.30pm departure would be away around 5pm, and then coaches would leave at around 15 minute intervals until finally the service car and sixth duplicate would invariably head north together at 6.30pm. The sight of two, or even three, Midland Red motorway coaches racing north in the third lane, nose to tail, was an awesome and somewhat frightening sight.

Drivers' tales of exceeding 100mph were commonplace and whilst impossible to verify, the unofficial record when I was there for the end-to-end dash was held by a Jamaican driver from Bearwood. He had that happy-go-lucky Caribbean disposition and seemed to come to work from a different direction every day. One Sunday morning he arrived in Digbeth at 10.10am, having left Victoria on time at 8.30am – a very creditable 1 hour and 40 minutes.

Buoyed by the success of its Birmingham-London service, a Nuneaton-Coventry-London service was introduced in September 1960 and a Birmingham-Worcester service was launched in July 1962 again on the opening day of that section of the M5 Motorway. Scheduled to take just 50 minutes, this service was even faster than the train.

With the increase of the legal maximum PSV dimensions to 36ft (11m) long and 8ft 2½in (2.5m) wide in August 1961, Midland Red set about building a vehicle to take full advantage of the new dimensions. Designated CM6T, these new coaches built on the CM5 experience.

They had a new-look front end and included a number of improvements. Passengers benefited from forced-air ventilation rather than hopper side windows. Drivers benefited from a Self Changing Gears semi-automatic gearbox and, given the extra length, the Traffic Manager benefited from an increased payload of 46 seats. The first CM6Ts entered service in February 1965 on the Birmingham-London service at about the same time as the service clocked up its millionth passenger.

Regrettably, the introduction of the national 70 miles per hour speed limit and the subsequent European regulatory requirement for new coaches to be speed limited to 100 kph (62.5 mph) coupled with the British Government's imposed outside lane ban on three and four lane motorways will prevent coaches ever travelling as quickly between the West Midlands and London again.

Express service deregulation came on 6th October 1980 and with it some serious competition for National Express and for the Scottish Bus Group's Citylink services. In response to these new challenges, National Express launched its up-market Rapide brand in November 1981. Rapide featured direct non-stop services, on-board toilets, videos, air-conditioning and hostesses serving refreshments, which was a step change in the customer offering.

One such new coaching entrant was British Coachways (BC), which was a consortium of established operators comprising Wallace

Posed here for a publicity photograph at Birmingham's Digbeth Coach Station, and facing the entrance rather than the exit, 4808 was the first Midland Red CM5T coach to carry fare-paying passengers. Built specifically for the Birmingham – London Motorway Express service which was launched on 2nd November 1959, the day that the M1 opened to traffic. These vehicles, which were high speed versions of the company's C5 coaches, were fitted with turbochargers and up-rated drive-lines. (BMMO, courtesy The Transport Museum Wythall)

Arnold of Leeds, Grey-Green of North London, Shearings of Altrincham, Morris Brothers of Swansea and Parks of Hamilton; each operator painted vehicles in a dedicated BC livery and the consortium offered a network of services at cheaper fares than National Express. However, a robust fares response from NE, and denial of access to London Victoria and Birmingham Digbeth coach stations in particular, meant that the consortium did not last long. Wallace Arnold and Grey-Green soon left the group to be replaced by Barton of Nottingham and Excelsior of Bournemouth but when the temporary BC London terminal was taken over by developers in October 1982 BC-branded operations ceased altogether. Nevertheless, some of the parties continued to offer their services jointly with National Express or became NE contractors.

Another new entrant was run by a brother and sister team, Brian Souter and Ann Gloag who launched express services between Scotland and London. With brother David doing the marketing and Ann's then husband, Robin, the maintenance, their Stagecoach operation was dismissed by the NBC and SBG establishments as a quirky upstart which wouldn't last five minutes. This was to be followed by a dawning realization that Brian and Ann knew exactly what they were doing and needed to be taken seriously. By then, however, they had built loyalty to their strong brand with its offer of cheap fares and on board food, which was prepared in Ann's kitchen by their parents. In 1982 they gambled £200,000 on the purchase of two new Neoplan Skyliner 75-seater coaches but within days they were helped by a lengthy rail strike, thus ensuring

that they were there to stay. It was only when Stagecoach was successful in the NBC privatization process in 1987 and had bought further bus companies from their management buy-out teams in 1989 that the decision was made to concentrate on buses and sell the express coach services to National Express who rebranded it Caledonian Express.

Express service deregulation also encouraged manufacturers to develop new double-deck coaches. Leyland decided to build one using an

Below: A pair of Midland Red CM5Ts speed south through Northamptonshire on the Birmingham-London Motorway Express service not long after the M1 opened. Motorway traffic was light in 1960, with traffic densities less than one fifth of those in 2010, while most family cars were barely capable of a top speed of 70mph. Initially, there were no crash barriers protecting bridges, nor in the central reservation and on this section there was no hard shoulder either, only a soft verge. (Ken Jubb)

Bottom: The prototype 50-seat Weymann bodied Leyland PDR1/1 coach, with a top speed of 48mph, was delivered in 1959 and used the M1 when it first opened. This example, capable of 64mph, is one of twenty-four further vehicles delivered to Ribble's Standerwick subsidiary, in 1960 and 1961. With a much longer journey than Midland Red, refreshments were served by stewardesses earning the vehicles their Gay Hostess title at a time when such a soubriquet was perfectly acceptable in everyday parlance. (David Powell)

Wessex was the first NBC Company to trial this prototype 69-seat ECW bodied Leyland Olympian T11 double-deck motorway coach, seen leaving Victoria in late summer 1982. None of the type were subsequently purchased for National Express duties. (Geoffrey Morant)

extended 11.3 metre Olympian chassis with an ECW body. National Express took delivery of the prototype in August 1982 and it did the rounds for evaluation. While this was a two-axle vehicle, Metro-Cammell-Weymann (MCW), the Birmingham-based bus and train manufacturer, opted for three axles with the potential for a smoother ride, when designing its Metroliner double-deck coach. The first Metroliners rolled off the production line in 1983 and NBC, deciding to put all of its National Express eggs into the MCW basket, took delivery of 127 of them for its Rapide network. A further twelve were delivered to the Scottish Bus Group and six were also supplied to Armstrong Galley (AG). AG was the coaching division of Tyne and Wear PTE, which in 1984 started its Non-Stop Clipper service to compete with the National Express 525 Rapide service on the Newcastle to London corridor. Whilst providing high standards of passenger comfort Metroliners did have their engineering weaknesses. As Midland Red had learnt when testing its CM5, the windscreen wipers struggled to stand up reliably to high-speed motorway operation and the angle drive was a weak point in the drive train. Armstrong Galley engineers became adept at anticipating the life of angle drives and would replace them one round trip ahead of projected failure – or so they claimed! Nor did the coaches stand up well to corrosion. The combination of winter

road salt with reduced air pressure in the vehicles' wake at speed and the Metroliner's all steel construction, resulted in serious rear upper-deck floor corrosion after a few years. However, after five years of intensive service most Metroliners would have already clocked up a million miles.

By 1989 National Express and Scottish Citylink had, one way or another, seen off all the serious express service competition. And so it remained until 2003, when Stagecoach re-entered the market with its megabus.com brand. This time, Stagecoach used a different business model relying entirely on internet ticket sales supplemented by walk-on fares and using yield management techniques pioneered by the discount airlines. In so doing, tickets could be offered from as little as £1, plus a booking fee. Buoyed by its UK success, Stagecoach is now also rapidly expanding megabus.com operations in the United States, with minimum fares starting at $1.

With the recent deregulation of international express coach services throughout the EU, it is likely that the market is about to enter another exciting new phase.

Above: Thanks to its distinctive and imaginative branding the megabus is an instantly recognisable feature of UK motorway travel, the bold pricing making car drivers and their passengers acutely aware of the difference in cost between private motoring and using these comfortable modern vehicles. (David Cole)

Below: The first USA megabus.com operations began in Chicago in April 2006. By 2012 the US network had carried 18 million passengers with 30 services operating from eight hubs and serving 80 cities. This Cummins-engined 13 metre tri-axle Van Hool TD95 is boarding passengers at Penn Station New York City in October 2008. (Stagecoach)

TIME FOR CHANGE – THE 1968 TRANSPORT ACT – BIRTH OF THE PTEs

The late 1960s and 1970s was a period when the entire bus industry struggled to keep afloat. Staff core terms and conditions were negotiated nationally in both the municipal and company sectors while shop-floor trade union militancy was on the rise. The grip held by the unions was not unique to the bus industry and the number of days lost annually through strikes in all sectors nationally increased four-fold from 5.7 million in 1962 to 23.9 million in 1972, before reducing to 5.3 million in 1982. By 2012 the annual number of days lost through industrial action had fallen to 1.4 million – the majority of which were in the public sector. The combined effects of plentiful alternative employment, inflation, union inflexibility and the inability to pay local market rates of pay left some operators struggling to retain sufficient staff to man their rotas with a resulting high incidence of lost mileage. Bus work, despite its inherent job satisfaction for those who enjoy working with people, has always suffered from its unattractive shift patterns and requirements to work evenings and weekends, when people most value their leisure time. The impact of the resultant poor service delivery, coupled with the increasing availability of mass-produced affordable private cars and the impact of a television set in every home meant that ridership declined at an alarming rate. Patronage on the nation's trams, trolleybuses and motorbuses fell by 21% from 1952 to 1962, 37% from 1962 to 1972, 30% from 1972 to 1982 and 15% from 1982 to 1992.

There was an inevitable air of realism at the highest levels in the industry. I recall being an enthusiastic young undergraduate applying to join the BET management training scheme in 1969. In those days before widespread use of computers and photocopiers, job applications were completed in long-hand and I committed the cardinal sin of failing to keep a copy of my submission. Some three months later when I was summoned to New Street Square in London to meet the recruitment panel I was reminded that in my application form I had

With 120 buses, West Bromwich was the smallest of the four municipal undertakings transferred to West Midlands PTE in October 1969. Many of its services were jointly operated with the neighbouring Birmingham, Walsall or Wolverhampton undertakings or with Midland Red. Like many municipals it standardized its fleet. This 1961 66-seat Metro-Cammell-bodied Daimler CVG6 is a typical example. When photographed in 1972, 229 had been transferred to Walsall and is working an ex-trolleybus route. (Geoffrey Morant)

given as a reason for my wanting to join the industry my belief that "it had a great future". The killer question was then put to me, "You don't really believe that do you, Mr Nash?" Unprepared for this challenge, I can recall quickly concluding that I could only say "Yes" since any other answer would only lead to further questions concerning why I had lied in my application. My youthful enthusiasm must have won the day as I was still offered the job on what had by then become the Provincial Omnibus Companies' training scheme, and was soon to be the National Bus Company training scheme.

The industry was reaching a critical state and something had to be done. The 1968 Transport Act was an attempt by the then Labour Government to find a remedy. The Act created the National Bus Company to run the Transport Holding Company fleets already in state ownership and the recently acquired BET Company operations. It also created Passenger Transport Authorities (PTAs) and Executives (PTEs) in four of the major Metropolitan areas: West Midlands, Merseyside, Manchester, and Tyneside. Their remit was to integrate local bus and rail services and to take over the municipal bus operations in their respective areas. To enable the PTAs to integrate services with the

National Bus Company they were empowered to make operating agreements with the local NBC subsidiaries. The idea that consolidating businesses to enable economies of scale which would achieve efficiency and improve productivity was fashionable throughout UK corporate business at that time (e.g. British Leyland) and there were many who believed that the PTEs would be the salvation of local bus networks in their conurbations.

The 1974 Local Government Act took the concept one stage further with the creation of the Metropolitan County Councils in each of the designated areas and the addition of three more: West and South Yorkshire, and Strathclyde in Scotland. These new authorities became the PTAs for their areas. Thus, in the major conurbations there was one unified transport, highways and economic and strategic planning authority controlled by local politicians who were elected to their positions and could be judged at the ballot box on their performance with the local transport network. This new arrangement was welcomed by the trade unions who were often in control of their local Labour parties and thus able to select and deselect the Labour candidates in local elections. But it was also resented by the Metropolitan District Authorities who disliked having a big brother Authority which was in a position to dictate what could and could not happen on their local patch. From the bus service perspective, and despite the disadvantage of the close relationship between trade unions and Labour elected members,

Sunderland Corporation's bus operation transferred to Tyneside PTE in April 1973, a year ahead of the formation of the Tyne & Wear Metropolitan Transport Authority. With the transfer came this 77-seat Roe bodied Daimler CRG6LX, one of 33 similar vehicles delivered in several batches between 1963 and 1966. (Geoffrey Morant)

Southport Corporation began tramway operation in 1900. Its first bus was purchased in 1924 and the undertaking survived for a further 50 years until, together with St Helens Corporation, it was absorbed into Merseyside PTE. Seen here in 1976, this was one of ten 1973 74-seat Alexander-bodied Leyland Atlantean AN68/1Rs. (Geoffrey Morant)

Manchester's Mancunian was a stylish vehicle of which 472 were ordered from 1965 onwards. This example, seen in SELNEC PTE colours loading in Piccadilly in 1972, is a 73-seat Park Royal-bodied Leyland Atlantean PDR1/1. Buses have now been displaced from this area of Piccadilly as part of a redesign to make way for the Metrolink trams. (Geoffrey Morant)

The out of line destination display spoils the otherwise smart appearance of this West Yorkshire Metro liveried ex-Bradford 76-seat Alexander-bodied Leyland Atlantean PDR2/1 seen here in 1976. (Geoffrey Morant)

51

The South Yorkshire PTE livery does not flatter this ex-Doncaster 74-seat Roe-bodied Daimler CRG6LX. Nevertheless, South Yorkshire's cheap fares policies help to ensure that it is carrying a good passenger load in this 1976 view. (Geoffrey Morant)

there were clear advantages in the PTA being able to specify and deliver bus priority measures to improve the reliability and efficiency of bus service delivery. Despite these benefits, as the figures above demonstrate, the hoped for turn round in patronage was never delivered. At best, all that the PTEs managed to achieve was a slight slowdown in ridership decline.

The PTAs and their PTEs soon proved that they were adept at developing proposals for grand projects. Tyneside promoted its rapid transit scheme and after skilful lobbying by politicians and PTE was able to secure a £35m government grant to convert and extend the North Tyneside loop railway to Metro operation. Competition between the PTEs for government funding was intense. South Yorkshire lobbied for its Sheffield Supertram and West Midlands argued for the Midland Metro line between Birmingham and Wolverhampton and all of these succeeded. However Manchester, with its PicVic scheme to provide an underground national rail link between its two main rail termini, was not, although its later Metrolink tram proposals were. Neither were Leeds' bid for trolleybuses nor the much more recent Merseyside tram proposals successful.

Eventually, In July 2012 the Department for Transport finally announced £173.5m funding towards an 8.7 mile trolley bus route in Leeds, scheduled to cost £250m and complete in 2018. New trolleybus systems don't come cheap!

The problem with most of these major investments was that they each provided a public transport "carrot", but neither the Authorities, nor the Government, were ever prepared to wield a car-restraint "stick" to prevent the eventual operating system becoming a drain on the public purse. In both Edinburgh and Manchester, when referenda on road pricing as part of a package to secure tram developments were put to the people, the results were a resounding "no" – but despite this the investment took place anyway.

In 1975, the Tyneside Metro nearly came to grief before it was half completed. The Government was running out of money and the scheme costs were escalating rapidly. To cap it all, the trade unions could not agree who should drive the trains with ASLEF, the NUR and the TGWU, who between them were going to lose 400 buses worth of work from the integration exercise, all demanding rights to the keys. At the height of the crisis David Howard, the Metro Project Director, told local journalists that if the project was cancelled he would use the already completed tunnels to grow mushrooms! The trade unions finally made an agreement at the eleventh hour with a deal which gave each a share of seats in the Metro

The Tyne & Wear Metro opened in 1980 and mostly used former railway track and stations but with a new Tyne bridge and tunnels in central Newcastle and Gateshead. The rolling stock is currently undergoing an extensive refurbishment and re-livery scheme which began in 2010 and is expected to continue until 2014. This view shows a scene amidst traditional railway architecture, and was taken in May 2003. (John Senior)

cabs. These rail-based projects are neither cheap to build nor operate. By way of example, when the Tyne and Wear Metro reaches its 40th anniversary in 2020, it alone will have consumed a billion pounds of public money.

Once the funding had been secured for a major project, then the lobbying immediately switched to new proposals within each area. Sunderland joined Tyneside PTA to become Tyne & Wear PTA in 1974 and so the agitation was for the Metro to be extended to Sunderland, the most populous of the Metropolitan Districts but the only one to not have a Metro presence. The argument ran that Sunderland was now paying Metro subsidies through its council taxes and so should have some Metro too. The plan was to run Metro over national rail tracks from Heworth to Sunderland and then extend it over a disused rail alignment to South Hylton, a small ex-pit village on the south bank of the river Wear. The South Hylton extension had little to do with demand, and everything to do with minimizing construction cost, given the available alignment. By coincidence, it was also the home of Malcolm Quailey, the leading Sunderland member on the PTA, who for several years had led the campaign for Metro to Sunderland. Sadly he was to die before the line to South Hylton was completed.

In South Yorkshire's case, once Supertram funding had been secured, the local political interest turned to the next largest borough, Doncaster. Here was a town with a proud trolleybus history so what better than to seek to reinstate trolleybus services. A Dennis Dominator double-deck bus was purchased in 1985, but instead of a conventional diesel engine it was equipped with a smaller diesel unit to enable it to crawl around unaided and an electric motor to be fed via overhead trolley poles. Several million pounds were then spent constructing a one mile test track, with turning loops at each end, at Sandal Beet alongside the straight, on Doncaster race course. The project worked well until the first meeting of the racing season, when it was discovered that the overhead support poles were obscuring the view of the start line from the Grandstand. So at further cost, the traction poles had to be moved to the other side of the test track to maintain the race-goers unrestricted vision. Despite all this expenditure, Doncaster's trolleybus

The result of a joint project with GEC, this demonstrator Dennis Dominator 80-seat Alexander-bodied trolleybus was delivered in 1985. The only one built, it is currently at the Sandtoft Trolleybus Museum. The overhead for the test line remained until 1994, when it was removed to storage. (Gary Nolan)

network never materialized and the promoters might have done well to ask themselves why trolleybuses had been withdrawn everywhere else in the UK, apart from the three enthusiast run transport museums.

These two examples show how, if Parliament creates local transport authorities with their own precepting powers they promote high visibility projects, which have more to do with civic pride and equity of provision than with affordable transport solutions. The penny seems now to have dropped and Integrated Transport Authorities no longer precept in their own right, but instead must persuade their Metropolitan District Authorities to fund their activities. Meanwhile, it has been left to those in the shire counties with less money to spend, like Cambridgeshire and South Hampshire, to be the first to implement more affordable bus solutions such as guided busways.

AND FERRIES TOO

Merseyside and Tyneside PTEs, also gained responsibility for operating important cross-river ferry services. It may have been that the previous operators, the Port Authorities, saw the opportunity to dispose of them as too good to miss. In Merseyside's case, responsibility for the Mersey Tunnels also passed to the PTE, but on Tyneside the tunnel staff managed to evade the PTE's clutches, although the PTA still had political control.

The cross-Tyne ferry between North and South Shields, close to the river's mouth, avoids a seven mile detour through the Tyne Tunnel which even then was renowned for congestion at peak periods and has only recently been dualled. The seven minute crossing was busy at peak times when shipyard workers would flock to it as they followed the work from one shipyard to another on either bank of the river. The PTE's ferry inheritance included the steam-powered Northumbrian vessel which could best be described as "clapped out" and an early decision of the PTA was to invest in a new vessel to serve the route. The PTE thought that ordering a ferry was much like ordering new buses and, without the aid of a marine architect, they placed a contract to build the vessel with Ryton Marine. Surprisingly, this was the only non-union shipyard on the Tyne and was one which had no previous experience of ferry-boat construction. The first sign of problems ahead was when the boat failed its first Plimsoll line test, necessitating some serious weight reduction in the superstructure before approval was given. The second was shortly after the launch in 1972 at which the vessel was named MV Freda Cunningham, by the wife of the then Chairman of the PTA, Councillor Andrew Cunningham. Cunningham was forced to resign as he became embroiled in the Poulson scandal. John Poulson was a prominent Yorkshire architect who won contracts with Newcastle and other councils to

Moored here at South Shields ferry pontoon landing in 1982, is the MV Freda Cunningham. This vessel was Tyneside PTE's first attempt at ferry specification, entering service in 1972 but surviving only four years in front line service. (Trevor Hall)

build new tower blocks in the 1960s. He gave bribes to T. Dan Smith, the leader of Newcastle City Council and to Andrew Cunningham, for which all three were imprisoned.

Thus Freda, the boat, became an enduring embarrassment, but as it was considered bad luck to rename a vessel, Freda Cunningham she remained. Once the vessel entered service, criticism became more vocal as she was less than reliable. One of the biggest problems was that ropes and other debris drifting in the tidal river became entwined in the conventional propellers, necessitating interruptions to the service while the boat was fixed. This did not go down well with the shipyard workers who relied on the ferry for their journey to and from work as replacement buses had to use the congested Tyne Tunnel which extended journey times by 40 minutes or more.

The second problem was one of capacity, since there were occasions when the flow of shipyard workers across the river was much higher than expected. (The PTE's planning department had conducted surveys of usage, to establish the size of vessel needed, but it seems that their sample had not picked up these exceptional movements). A twenty minute delay until the next sailing went down extremely badly with the workers who would have lost paid time going to work, and leisure time on their return. Added to all of this was the continual embarrassment of the vessel's name as a constant reminder of the man who had spectacularly fallen from grace. All in all it was not an auspicious start for Tyneside PTE's investment programme.

The ferry service was managed with the bus operations and a radio link was provided to the bus control room in Newcastle. Imagine his surprise, when the late-duty bus controller received a frantic message one evening in 1978 from the ferry night watchman, advising that the landing stage was sinking and that it was dragging Freda Cunningham down with it. Between them they decided that the only course of action was to release the mooring ropes and cut the boat adrift. The controller then raised the Tyne Pilots who went out to rescue the vessel and its sole crew member, the night watchman. The PTE's internal post-mortem concluded that the Port of Tyne Authority had engaged a new type of dredger to clear the channel which had managed to disturb the silt beneath part of the landing stage causing it to settle on the river bed at low tide at an angle. As the water rose, it entered one of the air vents and caused the pontoon to

flood and stay on the bottom, rather than float as it should have done. Needless to say the Port of Tyne Authority refused to accept any responsibility for the debacle. Aside from the disruption to service before the landing stage was serviceable again, there was also the small matter of a missing portable toilet cabin which had floated off the stage and out into the North Sea with the tide, never to be seen again.

Tyneside PTE had learnt the hard way that running buses was a piece of cake when compared with running ferries and it quickly persuaded the PTA to order a second ferry, and on this occasion to employ the services of a naval architect. The Shieldsman was built at Pembroke Dock and entered service in 1976. She was able to carry 350 passengers, could board passengers from either side and plied the Tyne for over 30 years, seventeen of which were on frontline service, four times longer than her infamous predecessor.

THE END OF AN ERA

The creation of the PTEs also meant the demise of no fewer than 34 municipal bus operations, as well as some changes in the National Bus Company map. The Newcastle, Leeds, Sheffield, Liverpool, Birmingham and Manchester municipal fleets dwarfed the other operations in their areas and in each case were larger than the combined size of the other incorporated fleets taken together. It was inevitable that over time they would come to dominate the way the businesses were run in each metropolitan area. Some of the original municipal operations were, by comparison, little gems in their own right and even in PTE control they consistently lost less mileage and received proportionately fewer passenger complaints. They also tended to charge lower fares before the inevitable political requirement to implement standard fares scales throughout the metropolitan area was implemented. These were the undertakings which were run like large family businesses – with all the joys and tensions evident in most family relationships.

South Shields was a typical example. Its services didn't stray far beyond the town boundary and the centre of social life was the club which was situated inside the depot. Outsiders were treated with suspicion until they had proved they were worthy of the employees' trust and the PTE quickly learnt that ideally the Divisional Manager needed to be, or to have previously been, "one of them". It always struck me as unusual that the

platform staffs were entirely white, Geordie males. Granted this was in the days before race and gender discrimination became a concern, but it was the more surprising because South Shields was a cosmopolitan town which proudly boasted one of the first mosques in the country. When I asked why this should be, the reply was something along the lines of, "If they don't apply, we can't appoint them" with an accompanying shrug of the shoulders.

In January 1975 Tyne & Wear PTE acquired the independent Economic service which ran two routes between Sunderland and South Shields via Whitburn. The operation was unusual in that it was a partnership between two proprietors, Anderson and Wilson. The

South Shields Corporation favoured Roe-bodied Daimler CVG6s like this fine 63-seat example laying over at South Shields Market Place in 1969. Wartime bomb damage permits a view of the Tyne which was soon to be obscured by Wouldhave House, a new three storey office block. In February 2012 the Council decided Wouldhave House was an eyesore and was to be demolished. (Omnibus Society collection - Peter Henson)

Below: This immaculate 1967 53-seat Plaxton-bodied AEC Reliance, below, belonged to the Anderson half of the Economic partnership. Seen here arriving in Sunderland in 1972, Northern's Park Lane Offices are clearly visible in the background. (Geoffrey Morant)

biggest stumbling block with the purchase was how they would divide the proceeds and the purchase consideration was eventually placed in a trust until, many months later, they finally agreed how to divide the spoils. With the operation came a number of conductresses, one

This 1957 Rotherham Corporation 59-seat Weymann-bodied Daimler CVG6 is seen leaving Doncaster for Sheffield, in 1967. Loading for Edlington is a Doncaster Corporation 45-seat Roe-bodied AEC Reliance. (Geoffrey Morant)

or two of whom were attractive young ladies. I well recall Gerry Graham, the Trade Union Secretary at South Shields telling me that they wouldn't last five minutes. Sure enough, he was right. After lurid tales of naked cavorting on the Leas at Marsden and a deputation of drivers' wives to see the Manager, the young ladies concerned soon resigned to take up alternative employment.

South Shields also employed an Inspector, Barry Dobson, who used to dress with military precision. You could see your reflection in his shoes and his expectations of the staff were of the highest order. Barry was generally tolerated but on one occasion a conductor somehow managed to push him off the platform of his bus as it left the terminus in South Shields Market Place. This occurred at the time when "On the Buses" was popular television viewing and the incident soon came to the ears of the Sun newspaper. For them, this was a perfect "Blakey" story. All they needed was a photograph of the man himself. As soon as I was alerted to the Sun's interest I told the Manager to get Barry out of town immediately. The paper's cameraman duly arrived that afternoon, but with the assistance of the trade union, Barry had been moved to a safe house and despite exhaustive enquiries the Sun never got its photograph, so couldn't run the story. Needless to say, Barry became a little more forgiving thereafter, much to the relief of both management and platform staff.

Rotherham was another typical municipal undertaking which disappeared when South Yorkshire PTE was created in 1974. Despite being larger than South Shields, with 135 vehicles, Gary Nolan tells of the family atmosphere which was still evident when he joined the PTE some four years later as a conductor. There was continuing staff resentment at Rotherham that Sheffield seemed to have both shorter and easier duties and better buses. One old driver once remarked to him that the next batch of new buses delivered to the PTE would be MCWs. When asked how he knew, the driver said that Sheffield would get the Metros, Doncaster would get the Weymanns and, as usual, Rotherham would get the Camels. (In those days Rotherham buses without power steering were called camels – because you had to stand up to steer them round a corner).

Gary remembers his days as a bus station inspector in Rotherham. The job involved regulating 120 departures an hour and, with the help of the radio system, second-guessing which buses might be so late that another should be inserted into the schedule to maintain the timetable, a job he found exacting but also rewarding when he guessed right. He recalls one day in 1982 when the wind was howling

through the bus station, which was situated beneath a multi storey car park and alongside the river Don. For some reason he decided to look over the parapet to check the height of the river, when a particularly strong gust removed his inspector's hat and he watched in horror as it spiralled in slow motion into the river below. Unfortunately for Gary the incident was also observed by about twenty drivers who were on their break. Having got over the initial embarrassment he completed his shift to find a group of laughing staff gathered round the Notice Board. Terry Broadhead, the depot cartoonist, had managed to capture the moment perfectly, with a drawing of Gary's hat floating down the Don, which he had depicted with ten illegal immigrants sitting inside it.

Changing the culture of an organization takes time, not least because the local practices and Spanish customs are handed down from one generation of staff to the next. This applies equally to the supervisors and to those they supervise. I was surprised when, in March 1974, I asked the Newcastle Chief Inspector, Tommy Pyburn, whether he could find me a couple of Inspectors for a particular job which needed supervision. He replied that it would be possible, but only if they were taken off checking duties, the easy way of responding to any additional demand.

When I asked what the problem was he explained that as it was the end of the holiday year, the inspectorate were short staffed as they were getting their sickness days in. Apparently, the inspectors' agreement in Newcastle provided for up to five days sickness each holiday year without loss of pay and over the years this had come to be interpreted as an extra holiday entitlement in the event that genuine sickness hadn't arisen. Fortunately, that wasn't a practice which occurred in either South Shields or Sunderland.

Gary Nolan also tells of more acceptable tricks of the trade which were handed down by the old hands. Harry Daglas was a long serving bus station inspector in Rotherham

The SELNEC logo was quite striking and instantly recognisable. In addition to orange, as here, blue, green and magenta colours were used to identify vehicles from the various divisions. Here a group of excited children board a vehicle from the coaching fleet under the watchful eye of an inspector. (Tony Young)

Opposite below: The facing view, taken in Ashton-under-Lyne's bus station in the early 'seventies, gives no indication that all three operators are now part of the recently formed SELNEC empire, with the Manchester Mancunian being flanked by a blue Roe-bodied Leyland Titan PD2 from Ashton and the red and white East Lancs-bodied PD2 from the Stockport fleets. Many of the smaller municipal operators taken into SELNEC had kept their vehicles commendably smart and it will be noticed that only the Manchester vehicle carries any external advertising. (John Senior)

Below: Stockport's Mersey Square, after North Western had become SELNEC Cheshire, and showing one of its ECW-bodied Bristol VRs loading at the lower right. To the left is one of Stockport's rare Longwell Green-bodied Leyland Titans, now carrying its new owner's logo in green on a white vinyl, denoting it was part of the southern fleet. The iconic Plaza cinema has since been completely refurbished and still provides an excellent viewpoint from its cafe windows although scenes such as this are now a distant memory. (John Senior)

who had a particular way of minimizing the number of driver requests for changeovers. His practice was to pre-arrange with the engineers the provision of the oldest, coldest, heaviest serviceable camel in the depot as the bus station spare. The vehicle would then be parked prominently in the designated spare stand for all the drivers to see. Harry reckoned that this was sufficient disincentive for all the drivers to persevere with what they had – unless the need for a changeover was entirely genuine. This particular practice was by no means confined to Rotherham and Inspectors elsewhere had sussed out that it was a good way of keeping the show on the road.

Perhaps the moral of all of these stories is that smaller operating units are easier to manage, if only because staffs get to know each other and their management so that, more often than not, they will willingly work together. These soft attributes are all intangibles, but together they contribute to better productivity and better customer service. This is a lesson which might be well remembered by those who attempt to micro-manage any "people business" from afar.

Such intangibles were also well understood by Bill Woolley, the Assistant Traffic Manager at North Western Road Car Company, who retired in 1971. Bill had held the company together as a succession of aspiring ex-Management Trainees passed through the Traffic Manager post on their way to higher things. NBC had decided that it would divest itself of certain of its operations in the Metropolitan areas if the PTAs wished to

Stockport Mersey Square was a busy hub for North Western services. This 1967 view includes a 75-seat Alexander-bodied Daimler CRG6LX, a 53-seat Willowbrook re-bodied Bristol K5G first registered in 1939, a 53-seat Willowbrook-bodied AEC Reliance and, to the rear, a 72-seat Park Royal bodied AEC Renown. (Photobus)

purchase them and so it was that those parts of the North Western company which traded largely within the Manchester PTA operating area (then known as SELNEC, which stood for South East Lancashire, North East Cheshire), were disposed of to the PTE. The deal had been done but not yet implemented when Bill retired and I remember attending his leaving do at the Alma Lodge Hotel on Buxton Road, Stockport. It came to speeches time and the Traffic Manager, Tom Dunstan, thanked Bill for all he had done for the Company and made a presentation to him.

When Bill stood up to reply, he thanked everyone for the support they had given him at the company over the years and wished them well for the future, particularly as many of them were about to become part of the SELNEC empire. He said that their situation reminded him of the ant climbing the elephant's leg. Half way up it paused for breath, looked up and pondered for a moment. It then said to itself, "Hmmm, the bigger the organization – the bigger the balls!" You weren't wrong, Bill!

The sale of the core of the North Western business in Greater Manchester also spelled the end of the company. This was a situation analogous to the sale of the core of Midland Red to the PTE in West Midlands, although the Midland Red Company was on its deathbed for a somewhat longer period.

James Isaac, Midland Red's TM when I was a trainee, was an excellent mentor who invited me to attend and observe many meetings with management and trade unions and would afterwards give me his time to ask questions and discuss the proceedings. It was Midland Red practice to have regular meetings with the senior Traffic Department personnel, including the Divisional Managers. A key agenda item was the financial performance of the business and I well remember Bert Sabell, the Central Divisional Traffic Manager, whose responsibilities covered many of the operations within the then West Midlands PTE area, arguing strongly but to no avail, that the apportionment of overheads between the Divisions was loaded against him and as a consequence, his financial performance was far better than the figures suggested. When 170 services, 413 buses and six garages were sold by Midland Red to the PTE in December 1973 for £3.6million, the remainder of the Company, which then resembled a Polo mint, with a hole in the middle, never recovered. This led me to the conclusion that perhaps Bert had been right all along.

PAY DAY

It has long been the tradition throughout British industry to employ manual workers on a weekly contract and to pay them in cash either on a Thursday or a Friday. For remote bus depots this entailed designated employees visiting the bank and collecting several thousand pounds as soon as the bank opened and then returning to the depot and making up individual pay packets with pay slips and cash so that staff could collect them later that day. The process was labour intensive and not without risk in the days before security couriers offered their services, as the bank run was a potential target for would be robbers. There was also the need to reconcile the pay-out and the inevitable accompanying panic when occasionally it didn't balance. It was therefore no surprise that operators started to move towards payment by credit transfer to employees' nominated bank or building society accounts during the 1970s and 1980s.

The risk of robbery was demonstrated in a different way at the Leamington depot of Midland Red in the early 1950s. Midland Red rigorously adhered to its financial control procedures and had audit systems in place to ensure they were maintained in practice; given the size of the Company, these procedures were essential. The arrangements for the payroll were clearly laid down. Every week, the Traffic Superintendent was required to send the summary net pay schedule for the depot to the Central Accounts department and a cheque was despatched in the post to him. The local branch of the bank had a list of three signatories from each company depot, two of whom had to be present to collect the cash. On the day in question, one of the signatories was on holiday and the Traffic Superintendent seized his chance. He told the third signatory that he was just popping home for something but would be back to collect him so that they could go to the bank together to cash the cheque. Time passed and the third signatory became concerned that there would be insufficient time to collect the cash and make up the pay packets before the queue were clamouring at the pay window for their money. He then made three phone calls. First, he rang the Traffic Superintendent's home number. The Superintendent's wife answered and to his surprise told him that she hadn't seen her husband since he had left for work some hours earlier. Secondly, he rang the

bank and was even more surprised to learn that the Traffic Superintendent had been in and had collected the cash! He asked how the TS could have done this, to be told that the TS had explained that one of his co-signatories was on holiday and that the other (him) was on the sick, and how he had to have the money or the staff wouldn't get paid. Thirdly, he rang Head Office in trepidation to explain what had happened. News of the heist quickly spread around the garage and one driver said that he had seen the Superintendent going into the railway station a little earlier that morning. This vital piece of information was relayed to the Police and the Traffic Superintendent was arrested on his arrival in London, with all the money, save his train fare, intact.

Despite the obvious attractions to employers of credit transfer payments, there was often trade union resistance to such a proposition. This was invariably because some employees didn't want their wives to know how much they earned, preferring instead to take home the cash having first "top sliced" their spending money from the net pay.

Jim Hulme tells of his early days in the industry when he was a junior clerk at Blackburn Corporation Transport. The storekeeper occasionally gave Jim a blank pay slip and then told him precisely how he wanted it completed. This made no sense to Jim, but as the new kid on the block, he didn't dare ask why he was required to do this. Some while later he discovered the answer. The storekeeper regularly did a driving shift at weekends and his wife was also a conductress for the same undertaking. Jim overheard the storekeeper's wife at one function, commenting to the Traffic Superintendent that she was pleased that he could employ her husband on the road at weekends but she did think it unfair that he was being paid considerably less than the other drivers for doing so!

I ran into difficulties of a similar nature when we were short of drivers in Newcastle in the mid-1970s. We regularly advertised for drivers in the Newcastle Evening Chronicle and I wanted to include average earnings, which were considerably higher than basic pay, as part of our recruitment message. This met with stiff resistance from the trade union, who were fearful some drivers' wives would read the paper and find out just how much their

Newcastle Corporation standardized on Alexander-bodied Leyland Atlanteans throughout the 1960s, though there were also some bodied by Weymann's and amongst the last built before the Addlestone-based company closed in 1966. This example, seen operating one of the cross-Tyne services jointly worked with Gateshead and District in May 1977, was one of 40 delivered in 1969/70. A 78-seat Alexander J type Leyland PDR2/1, it features dual-doors, the long panoramic windows first specified by Edinburgh Corporation, and a nearside staircase. (Geoffrey Morant)

men folk were actually earning. When I was threatened with a stoppage if I went ahead, I naively told the trade union that if they did that I would be happy to explain to the local media the real reason for the dispute, only for them to respond that they would sharply find another and less embarrassing reason for walking out if I went ahead!

Les Warneford fared rather better at the time he gained responsibility for the Crewe and Etruria operations of Crosville England in 1989 when the then owners, Drawlane, decided to split up the company and transfer these two garages to their sister Midland Red North subsidiary based in Cannock, where Les was Managing Director at the time. Les told me that he received a phone call one morning advising him of his additional responsibilities and duly set off for Crewe to take a look at his inheritance. On arrival, he discovered that there were no buses in the garage, which was on the same site as Crewe bus station. When he asked why, the staff told him that they understood that the depot had been sold for redevelopment and they had therefore removed the buses to a temporary site on the edge of town. Les told them to bring them straight back again – a decision which has stood the test of time, since Crewe bus garage remains standing at the time of writing. It is however empty as current operator, Arriva, has moved the vehicles to new premises in nearby Winsford – in readiness for that eventual redevelopment.

Les immediately decided that it was time that the ex-Crosville staff moved on to the same credit transfer payroll arrangements as the rest of the Midland Red North operations. He met the drivers' trades union to tell them that they now worked for him at Midland Red North and advised them of his intention to pay them by credit transfer. Perhaps it was because Crewe was a railway town, but the trade union there were untypically robust for a shire town of its size and firmly told Les that he couldn't do that because of the Truck Acts of 1831. These had never been repealed, giving them a legal right to be paid in cash which they would not concede. Les reflected for a moment and then told them that they were indeed right. He would continue to pay them in cash – but they would have to come to Cannock each week to collect their pay packets. The reaction from the other side of the table was somewhat less than cordial – but credit transfer was duly implemented.

Les also commented that staff attitudes at Crewe's Etruria outstation, despite being only fourteen miles away, could not have been more

NBC split up the Crosville Company before privatization. The English operations were purchased by ATL who sold to Drawlane in 1989. Drawlane further divided the business, managing Crewe and Etruria from its Midland Red North company based at Cannock. Pictured in Crewe bus station, is this 1980 74-seat ECW-bodied Bristol VRT/SL3. The two parts of Crosville are now re-united under Arriva ownership. (Ken Sutton)

Seen below with Crosville in earlier and better days this former North Western Daimler Fleetline with Alexander low-height body was operating from Manchester's Piccadilly bus station to Macclesfield where it would be based in the old North Western depot. Note the contrast in body styles with the Newcastle vehicle, opposite, whereby the low height, smaller windows and location of the staircase in its more usual position on the offside produce a very different outline. (John Senior)

different. On his first visit there he was again confronted with an empty depot but the six allocated buses started running in just after 6.00pm. He held an impromptu meeting with the staff in the shed which served as the office and mess room and asked whether there was anything they needed. They told him that the job was fine but the shed could really do with a makeover. Les got out his wallet and gave them £200 in cash, telling them to get down to B & Q and buy whatever they needed. He was pleasantly surprised that on his next visit the place had been transformed with a new coat of paint and curtains at the windows, which the drivers' wives had installed to make the place feel more like home.

Double-deck one-person-operation only became lawful in 1965 and until the 1970s the majority of bus services were crew-operated. As a consequence, the interaction between driver and conductor, or conductress, sometimes created an additional management challenge, not found today. Crew operation required teamwork between the platform and the cab, the success of which depended on the personal relationship between the driver and his conductor or conductress. I can recall working with drivers who were a pleasure to be with – friendly, skilled drivers who regulated their speed in accordance with your workload while at the same time maintaining the schedule. Others could be taciturn, or had heavy right feet and would throw you all over the bus. If a crew worked well together they could make life easy for their passengers and fellow crews or, in a few cases, the very opposite as some of the following anecdotes illustrate.

There were advantages and disadvantages of regular crew pairings and of working the same duty for a week. A paired crew got to know how each other worked – particularly important when it came to bell ringing on an open platform double-decker if both safety and tight schedules were to be maintained. Provided they got on well together, it could aid

staff retention but if they did not, it could lead to all sorts of friction. Becoming familiar with passengers could also improve customer service and help catch habitual fares dodgers, but over familiarity might also lead to complaints, and risked revenue if some passengers were allowed to ride at "mate's rates".

Familiarity could also lead to crews occasionally antagonizing regular passengers as Douglas Bailey recalls. He told me how he managed to cool the ardour of one young Romeo, when working the last bus to Darcy Lever on service 14 for a week as a crew driver in Bolton. On the Monday night, Douglas noticed that when they got to the outer terminus there was a young lad who was escorting his young lady home. The couple would spend the layover time locked in a passionate embrace in the bus shelter and then when Douglas started the engine and received the starting signal he would see a blur jump on to the bus through his nearside mirror just as they started to move off. Farewell complete, the young man had joined Douglas and his mate

Bolton Corporation ran a fleet of 270 buses when it purchased seven of these 74-seat Metro-Cammell-bodied Daimler CVG6's in 1958. Was Romeo going to catch this one – probably not if Douglas Bailey could help it! (Roy Marshall)

for the ride back to town. The same routine was repeated on the Tuesday and the Wednesday. On the Thursday, Douglas confided to his mate that he had worked out how he was going to catch the young man out that night, and said, "When we get to the terminus, you come round to the cab with me." When 11.15pm came, Douglas released the handbrake and the bus started to roll silently away. As it gathered speed, Douglas dropped it into third gear and the engine came to life. At the next stop his conductor returned to the platform and they continued their journey as normal. Douglas said that on the Friday his young male passenger glared at him when boarding and if looks could kill, he would have died in the cab, right there and then. Come the terminus, the young Romeo gave his girlfriend a quick goodnight kiss and leapt straight back on the bus. He wasn't going to walk home as he had to the previous night!

Romance was also a possibility if drivers and conductresses were regularly paired, when they might occasionally get on too well together. Eric Hutchinson told me of his early days at Venture Transport in Consett, where he was taught the ropes by General Manager Leslie Graham. He recalled that during a meal break at Consett Bus Station, one particular crew were unable to contain their amorous desires and slipped round the back of the canteen to pursue their illicit liaison in what they thought was absolute privacy. Unbeknown to them, they were observed by an elderly lady from the bedroom window of a neighbouring property. She held Venture Transport entirely responsible for their gymnastics and promptly rang the General Manager to complain vehemently. At interview, the crew sheepishly admitted their activities leaving Leslie Graham no option but to summarily dismiss them both for the capital offence of fornication in the Company's uniform.

As well as the separate responsibilities assigned to drivers and conductors there was also an informal understanding that the conductor was expected to buy the teas at layover time. This widespread practice must have had something to do with the fact that he was handling the Company's money and drivers therefore felt that their conductors should be able to generate their own sales commission. Mark Howarth tells of his days at Midland Red, when as a management trainee, he managed to elevate the layover cuppa to a whole new level.

During the early 1970s, Midland Red like most operators, struggled with platform staff shortages. Management trainees were expected to get behind the wheel outside office hours and help keep the show on the road. Saturday late turns were always the most difficult to cover, just as they are today, and Mark was able to take his pick from a number of duties at a number of depots. He opted for one of the few duties at Bromsgrove which didn't involve ploughing up and down on the 144 Birmingham-Worcester-Malverns service. With his regular conductor he spent every Saturday afternoon and evening working the 339 service between Bromsgrove and Stratford, which also included, and this was his reason for doing it, a trip on the 525 service from Stratford to Chipping Campden and return. The scheduled arrival in the Cotswolds market town was 3.30pm which was followed by a paid break of 45 minutes – perfect timing for afternoon tea. As they entered the town, Mark would slow down his D9 double-deck to let his conductor alight at the tea shop, would close the platform doors, proceed to the terminus and after setting down any passengers park his bus up in the High Street. He would then saunter back to the tea shop by which time his conductor would be already seated at a table in the window with a

This immaculate Venture Transport 51-seat Alexander Y type Leyland PSU3/4R was new in 1968. The Venture Transport offices and the cross above the church tower overlook this 1968 scene in Consett bus station. Venture was acquired by Northern in 1970. (Geoffrey Morant)

Gone for a cream tea? A few years before the story told on the previous page, a damp 1967 view of the same Chipping Campden parking place with a Bromsgrove garage D9 awaiting return to Stratford via Mickleton. (Geoffrey Morant)

New in 1958, this 73-seat Burlingham-bodied Leyland PD3/4 is working the Newcastle, Sunderland, and Hartlepool service 40 a decade later. Sunderland District was a Northern subsidiary and most of the group's double-deckers sported permanent "Shop at Binns" frontal advertisements at that time. (Roy Marshall)

full cream tea for two. Life for a management trainee doesn't get much better than being paid to enjoy a free Cotswold cream tea in picturesque surroundings!

Ron Davies was another member of the office staff who was expected to do a shift behind the wheel on a Saturday. At the time Ron worked for Sunderland District Omnibus Company (SDO) which was one of the Northern General subsidiary companies. He reported for duty on one occasion to be told that his conductor was newly recruited and was asked to keep an eye on him – a process we now call mentoring. The duty involved working the Newcastle-Sunderland-Hartlepool service 40 and on their first arrival at Worswick Street Bus Station

in Newcastle, Ron told the conductor to chock the bus. Confused by this instruction, Ron had to explain to him that as the departure bays were on a steep slope, it was the conductor's job to pick up a brass chock and place it behind the nearside rear wheel as a safety measure in case the handbrake proved unable to hold the vehicle. Time to go and Ron told the conductor to remove the chock before giving him the starting signal. On arrival in Hartlepool they were ready for a cup of tea, when the conductor asked Ron whether he should again chock the bus – and waved his souvenir from Worswick Street in Ron's direction. Ron calmly explained that the chock should have been left in Newcastle for the use of the next bus and that

Northern General's Worswick St Bus Station was built on a slope which is why buses were always chocked. A 1969 78-seat Alexander-bodied Daimler CRG6LX is nearest the camera in this scene which includes one of 50 Leyland-engined RMF 72-seat Routemasters bodied by Park Royal – the only new RM sales outside the London area. Also on view are Sunderland District and Northern Metro-Cammell bodied Leyland Atlanteans. (Newcastle Central Libraries)

the conductor might now find himself in trouble. His conductor was somewhat crestfallen as they set off back to Newcastle, perhaps fearing that his career with SDO might be prematurely terminated. On arrival in Worswick Street for the second time, Ron asked his conductor to again chock the bus. To Ron's surprise the reply was that he couldn't. Further questioning revealed that he didn't have it any more and had decided to jettison the evidence somewhere near Boldon Colliery by throwing the offending chock over a hedge and into a field.

Portsmouth Corporation's full title was the City of Portsmouth Passenger Transport Department (or CPPTD to give it its rather long abbreviated title). At Portsmouth, crews were regularly paired and worked the same duty for a week. As a student seasonal conductor there, I was assigned to the spare list, but occasionally clicked for a duty for a week when a regular

conductor was on leave. I recall working with one driver, who habitually set off without the starting signal. I knew that I was quick on the bell so I became increasingly annoyed by his antics, which were potentially dangerous. At the start of the Tuesday duty I asked him to wait for the bell before setting off. I asked him again on the Wednesday but it made no appreciable difference. On the Thursday, a chance to make my point duly arrived. At St Mary's Church on Fratton Road, I helped a young mum off the bus. I unfolded her pushchair on the pavement and then retreated behind the vehicle, out of the mirror sightlines. Sure enough, he set off without me. I patiently waited five minutes for the next bus and eventually, three or four stops down the road at North End, I found my bus waiting for me with an Inspector in attendance. I explained that I had alighted to help a lady with a pushchair and that the bell must have been rung by someone else. I am not sure what explanation the driver gave, but on the Friday his habit of departing prematurely was miraculously cured.

Typical of many provincial cities, Portsmouth had just two bus operators; in this case the

Corporation and Southdown, which ran most of the out of town services. In July 1946 after a referendum in the city and then Parliamentary approval, a Joint Agreement was signed whereby each would be entitled to an agreed percentage of pooled revenue and mileage. The agreement covered an area of 127 square miles including much of south-east Hampshire and survived with some amendment until outlawed by the 1985 Transport Act. The agreement required that each year an audit would take place and one party would take over one or more of the other's services for a short period in order to "run off" any excess mileage. This long standing agreement, which also meant shared staff buses, was probably the reason that Corporation and Southdown crews based in the city, worked well together on the road.

However, there was one crew, the Dart brothers, who were disliked throughout the Corporation's North End depot. Their crime was to ensure that everyone else always did the work. The geography of Portsea Island meant that there were just two main corridors where many services plied the same two routes. When busy, most crews played the game and we engaged in skip stop operation whenever the

opportunity arose, but not the Darts who would appear from nowhere behind you and then stick to your rear platform like glue.

Southdown's service 31 between Portsmouth and Brighton ran every fifteen minutes and despite the Joint Agreement was scheduled just two minutes ahead of the Corporation's 148A/B services to Leigh Park, which together also ran every fifteen minutes. They shared the same route from Commercial Road, Portsmouth to Bedhampton, a distance of some eight miles. Southdown had two garages in the city, at Hilsea and Hyde Park Road, and the service 31 crews based there took their fair share of the graft on the main drag. The crews working the 31 from Chichester garage however, were a different kettle of fish and many of them had been trained in the Dart school of bus operation.

On one busy day in August 1969, the inevitable happened. A service 31 crew from Chichester was scheduled two minutes in front of a 148A to Leigh Park manned by the Dart brothers. Cosham Red Lion was the last major pick up point on both services where a large percentage of the waiting passengers who were for Farlington or Bedhampton could catch either bus. The approach to this stop was preceded by two large roundabouts.

As they approached the second roundabout, the 31 was in front with the Darts in its slip stream, as they had been since leaving Commercial Road. No surprise there then.

Southdown service 147 was a 20 mile circumnavigation of Langstone Harbour from Hayling Island to Southsea. However, in this April 1968 view it is being worked by Portsmouth 120, a 1958 56-seat Metro-Cammell-bodied Leyland PD2/40 running balancing mileage to satisfy the terms of the Joint Agreement. (Geoffrey Morant)

The Chichester driver, upon reaching the second exit of the second roundabout, sized up the length of the Red Lion queue just fifty metres away and opted to miss the third exit and continue circling the roundabout – only to be followed by the Darts. He obviously didn't know the Dart brothers like we all did. It wasn't until they were on their second lap of the roundabout, that they were joined by a police Panda car with its siren blaring. The Chichester driver decided that he had pushed his luck as far as he could and pulled onto the stop, with the Darts tucked in behind. I can't help feeling that had it not been for that police intervention, they might still be there now!

This culture of work avoidance was more commonly directed at passengers, where some crews took a perverse delight in making life difficult for the very people who paid their wages. Examples of drivers who would not see "runners" by ensuring their eyes were glued to the offside rear view mirror as they drove away from stops, were common. Instances of this nature tended to be opportunistic, but a few drivers deliberately set out to confound their passengers. Brian Souter tells of his days as a rookie conductor working for Central SMT at East Kilbride, when he was conducting to pay his way through University. He recalls working with one particular driver on a service which ran from a relatively affluent estate to town via the local rail station enabling passengers to commute by rail into central Glasgow. Before starting duty the driver asked Brian whether they should run early or late, to which Brian asked why they couldn't just run to time. "No laddie, you don't understand", he was told. "If we run early they will miss us altogether and if we run late, they will catch us but they will miss their train".

Fortunately that mentality was the exception rather than the rule and in times of difficulty the majority of staff would throw away the rule book to do their best to deliver services. David Humphrey cites one such example from his early days in management at the Bristol Omnibus Company. His story goes like this:

"One morning after a heavy snowfall, I went to catch my bus to work from the terminus as usual. The driver was having some difficulty with his ticket machine: the motorized Setright wouldn't work because it was too cold for the motor to turn. I offered to conduct the bus and the driver gratefully handed me the machine and its emergency handle, and off we went.

"Progress was painfully slow due to badly parked cars and deep piles of snow alongside the road, and we were soon overwhelmed with passengers. The driver was happy to take all comers, and with about 40 people standing on a 44-seat single-decker (licensed to carry 8 standing passengers!), a very sticky ticket machine, and a very rusty conductor, it was quite a while before I managed to get back down to the front platform. Upon arrival, I saw a green body panel resting against the front bulkhead. "What's that?" said I. "Oh, didn't you notice? We had a little accident back there, and a car knocked the front offside corner panel off the bus. I thought I had better take it back in for repair!" After finishing the trip into the city centre, I emptied my pockets of a large quantity of cash, and made an attempt to cash up his waybill. I said if there was any discrepancy he should let me know. He thanked me for my help, and I heard no more. All this was in the context of a very strong and sometimes hostile trade union environment in which management were not allowed to drive or conduct buses and every rule was strictly adhered to, but my mate and I just got on with it. It was all very amicable, and there was no subsequent peep of objection from anywhere."

One of the duties often assigned to student conductors in Portsmouth was working the open-top seafront service which ran from Clarence Pier to the Hayling Island Ferry terminal at Eastney via South Parade Pier. The service was provided with three elderly Leyland TD4 double-deckers whose tops had been removed and which had to be changed over for conventional double-deck vehicles whenever it rained. To me, dealing exclusively with holidaymakers, it didn't constitute proper bus work although it did have its amusing moments. On one occasion I took the fares from a Brummie couple who had just come along for the ride, when I was asked how they might get to "Bongor Reggis". This beat me for a moment, so I asked how they had heard of it, to be told that they had seen it on the destination of a bus at South Parade Pier. The penny then dropped. They had seen a Southdown service 31 which was terminating at Bognor Regis.

On another occasion the American aircraft carrier USS Enterprise was paying a goodwill visit to Portsmouth with a complement of 5000 men, a large proportion of whom had been granted shore leave. We left Clarence Pier with a full load on this particular evening and when I went upstairs to collect the fares I knew that I would have to work fast to get the fares in before we reached South Parade Pier but I needn't have worried. The back seat was occupied by an American sailor who was accompanied by a rather tarty young lady he had obviously met since coming ashore. (I was to later learn that a lot of good time girls especially made the train journey down from London when the American fleet was in). He asked me what the fare was to South Parade Pier and I told him that it was 4d (2p). "Only fourpence", he exclaimed in total disbelief,

"In that case, I'll pay for the whole bus" and proffered a £5 note. I didn't argue and ran him off 26, 4d tickets, and holding tightly onto the note, so that it didn't blow away in the evening air, I gave him his change. When the other top deck passengers alighted and offered their fares, I told them that they had had a free ride," courtesy of the American Navy".

Above: Between 1958 and 1967, Southdown purchased 293 69-seat Northern Counties- bodied Leyland PD3s. Pictured at Southsea in September 1964, this 1959 PD3/4 example is arriving from Brighton, a scheduled journey of 3hrs 58mins – 22 minutes quicker than today's Coastliner 700 service. (Roy Marshall)

This 1935 50-seat English Electric-bodied Leyland TD4, seen at South Parade Pier in September 1967, was converted to open top in 1955. Withdrawn from service in 1971, it is now owned by Portsmouth Museums. (Roy Marshall)

LONG SERVICE

The bus industry tends to employ two sorts of drivers. There are those who are recruited but are off to pastures new within a couple of years. These tend to be the people who don't like the shift patterns or don't enjoy dealing with the public. Then there are those who grow to love the job and make bus work their career. Attitudes to employment have changed over the years and nowadays many youngsters tend to have no great loyalty to their current employer, although job security is becoming more highly prized in the current economic climate. Long service should be celebrated and most companies do so by inviting employees who have passed significant milestones to awards evenings where they and their partners are treated to dinner and have the chance to chat with senior management "off the job".

Of course, it is sometimes argued that you can't teach old dogs new tricks and that some long serving employees are often the worst ambassadors for the business. My experience is that such employees are the exception rather than the rule and are usually to be found only in poorly managed undertakings. With the advent of the driver's CPC and the requirement for 35 hours certified training every five years, there is now no reason why such liabilities cannot be turned into assets. Courtesy of Brussels, continuous professional development has finally arrived in the bus industry!

It is invariably the longer serving staff who can be relied upon to keep the show on the road when things unexpectedly go wrong; the relationships they form with their customers and work colleagues are the mystery ingredient which often accompanies excellent customer service. Andrew Dyer values the importance of long service to the industry and tells three very different tales about characters that in their own way provide the backbone to the business. His first relates to the early days of deregulation when he was at Cheltenham. Over to you, Andrew:

"As I write this, Rita Hart is Cheltenham's longest serving bus driver and certainly one of the depot's personalities. She has probably never forgiven me for the April fool joke she fell for in 1987 just after privatization.

"All the Cheltenham drivers had just been given smart new uniform with burgundy jackets and grey trousers. In the early hours of 1 April I posted a notice to staff to say that drivers would in future be expected to wear burgundy-coloured uniform shoes to match the new jackets. Due to financial cutbacks,

Sold to its management team in October 1986, the Cheltenham and Gloucester Omnibus Company Ltd was the third NBC privatization sale. Seen in Cheltenham eleven months later, resplendent in new livery, is this 1975 52-seat Leyland National. The Bristol VRT behind it was originally in the Bristol Company's Gloucester fleet, and had thereby escaped the standard NBC apple green livery. (Roy Marshall)

the notice said, staff would have to purchase these shoes themselves. As the drivers booked on for their early shifts they all had a chuckle, except Rita who made a beeline for the Union Branch Secretary accusing him of being useless and letting "that Dyer" get away with murder. When his response was "look at the date on the notice Rita", her reply was apparently "I don't give a **** what the date on the notice is, you get upstairs and sort that management out!" Later that afternoon when she had finished her shift, there was a knock on my office door. "I suppose you think you're funny" said Rita's voice. "They're all taking the mickey out of me!" I am delighted to say that Rita and I have been friends ever since."

His second story relates to an individual who Andrew believes could be the industry's longest serving employee. If you think he's wrong, then please tell Andrew, not me!

"On 11th August 2012, Neville Gosling completed 60 years continuous full-time employment with Stagecoach and its predecessors at Winchester. Employed as a junior clerk in 1952 he progressed to depot cashier where his able assistant was Tiddles the depot cat, who had adopted the cash office! Normally a popular figure, Tiddles nearly got Neville lynched one day as he was counting

out cash for wages. One nimble leap was all it took to get from floor to counter, except that he landed on a pile of £1 and ten shilling notes. Cat and notes skidded along the counter creating chaos and the late payment of drivers' wages!

"In the early 1990s cash counting was centralized but Neville elected to stay in Winchester as a cleaner where he remains at the time of writing. Having exceeded 50 years service Neville and his daughter attend every staff long service dinner and he really is "Father of the House". I have yet to hear of anyone else with 60 years continuous full-time service in the industry. Is this a record? Congratulations Neville!"

And finally, Andrew tells of one particular conductress who became a national celebrity for completing over fifty years service on one and the same route, as he now explains:

"I think it is fair to describe Phyllis Maycock as one of my heroines! For 51 years from 1942 to 1993 she conducted the same bus route from Piddington to Oxford via the Otmoor villages, run by Charlton-on-Otmoor Services. Phyl, as everyone knew her, was a battleaxe bus conductress with a heart of gold and not only knew everyone in the villages, but also their friends and relatives who made occasional visits by bus. At the tender age of 16, I got a school holiday job with Charlton Services and Phyl taught me to be a bus conductor. I then conducted the route while she was on holiday. The first day was not easy. People would just sit and hold out their money while they gossiped

When this bus was delivered new to Hants and Dorset in 1967, Neville Gosling had already completed 15 years service with the Company. A 70-seat ECW-bodied Bristol FLF6L, it is seen leaving Broadway, Winchester, for Southampton in February 1968. Two of R. Chisnell & Sons (King Alfred) buses are just visible behind it. (Geoffrey Morant)

Many bus operators celebrate staff long service with an annual awards evening. This 2009 gathering could be anywhere the UK, but is actually in South Wales where eleven members of Stagecoach staff were celebrating a combined 360 years service with the Company and its predecessors. (Stagecoach)

Foot of page: To achieve 51 years service is remarkable. To do so on just one bus service deserves a medal. Phyllis Maycock, MBE, poses for the press in 1993 on the steps of Charlton-on-Otmoor Services' Piddington to Oxford service. The vehicle is a 1977 55-seat Plaxton-bodied Leyland Leopard. (Bicester Advertiser)

about village events. When I asked "Where to" the reply was simply "Well Phyl knows"!

"Wednesday was Oxford market day and so the busiest day of the week. On my first Wednesday conducting the 5.10pm bus from Oxford we had six standing passengers on the elderly ex-London Transport RT. After work, I saw Phyl in the village pub. She used to say that she was going to Ourgate and Paint'n for her holidays meaning that she was staying at home to do decorating! "How're you getting on boy?" I was asked. "Oh Phyl, the 5.10 was really full, I had six standing" I replied. "FULL? You call that full?" came the quick response. "I'll tell you what's full". She then proceeded to tell this story from 1946. The route went past a barracks near Bicester where Army personnel were stationed while they waited to be demobbed. As a result they went into Oxford drinking on a Saturday night and caught the last bus back to the camp.

"In Phyl's own words… 'During the war nobody bothered you as long as you got people to where they wanted to go, but afterwards rules and regulations started to be enforced. Normally we'd have two buses on the last trip, but on this particular night one had broken down and so I had to manage with one bus. It was packed with drunken squaddies and I thought we were a bit full cos' as we went round the corner out of Gloucester Green Bus Station, the platform scraped the ground! Round in Beaumont Street by the Ashmolean [museum] the police stopped us. "You're overloaded" said this jumped-up young copper "I'll have to report you". "Well, it's like this my duck", I said. "Either I can take them back to camp or I can throw them off the bus here and you can stop them going round Oxford wrecking the place".

He paused to take a look at the state of the passengers, and we were soon sent on our way! I thought I would just count them as they got off to see how full we were …. and we only had 109 on a 56 seat decker!'

"On her retirement a local parish council nominated Phyl for the 1994 New Year's Honours list and she was awarded the MBE for services to the community. As a result she was the subject of an episode of 'This is Your Life'. One of the story lines was 'the boy she taught to be a bus conductor is now the MD of a bus company' and I had the honour of going through those doors with Michael Aspel to pay tribute to her.

"Sadly Phyllis died in 2005 in Charlton-on-Otmoor where she had been born. Hundreds of well-wishers crowded into the village church for the funeral. Just before the service started I heard a woman in the pew behind me say 'Isn't the church full!' I could immediately hear Phyl's voice in my head. 'FULL? Do you call this full? You could fit at least another 20 standing at the back!'

STOP THIEF!

Most people are basically honest. Others will commit fraud if they believe that there is little chance of detection, particularly if they regard the theft as trivial. Then there is a small hard-core that will always attempt to beat any system. These are the ones who are persistently dishonest or who are looking for an intellectual challenge. Overlaying these attitudes is the perception of what is deemed acceptable by one's peers. Most of us think it is fair game to pilfer pens from the office, so long as it's just the one that is in your jacket pocket.

In the days of crewed bus operation, "fiddling" the tea money would be widely accepted amongst platform staff as fair game. That doesn't make the practice right and drawing a line between petty pilfering and systematic theft is impossible. Passenger and staff attitudes are also coloured by their perception of the sanctions which might apply if "caught in the act", which is why any instance of staff theft is usually regarded to be a dismissible offence. Crucially, the design of a fares collection system also influences how many customers or employees will try to exploit it.

The rush to convert services to one-person operation in the late 1960s and 1970s put a spotlight on the delays caused by the existing fares collection systems. Many municipal operators opted to adopt fare boxes, whereby passengers were required to put the correct fare into the box where it was held securely behind glass. The driver, once satisfied that it was correct, would release the coins into the fares vault. Such systems remove the driver's accountability for his takings and in so doing, increase his incentive to steal the cash. In order to minimize these risks, the standing rule where fare boxes were deployed was that drivers must under no circumstances handle cash.

"No change" systems are passenger-unfriendly and fare boxes have largely disappeared, although they can still be found in the West Midlands, Edinburgh, Glasgow, Aberdeen, Cardiff, Nottingham and a handful of other cities. In central London, Transport for London (TfL) has taken this one stage further by following the continental practice of requiring their cash passengers to use exact fare on-street ticket machines in the central area. However, TfL has more recently announced that from April 2013 these machines will be removed and passengers may once more

In the 1970s some municipal operators introduced fare boxes in order to speed up boarding on one-person buses. While eliminating change-giving saved time, passengers who didn't know their exact fare were disadvantaged. Most operators later abandoned the system. Travel Coventry was an exception, as seen on the platform of this 72-seat Wright bodied Volvo B7TL waiting time in Hales Street, Coventry in September 2012. (Peter Nash)

pay the driver. Gary Nolan tells of one long-serving Rotherham driver who one Monday morning had to deal with a child who had somehow managed to put both his dinner money and his fare into the fares box. There was no way of recovering the money and the lad was distraught. The driver decided to break all the rules and recover the dinner money from the following boarding passengers, before the balance went into the vault. He then spent the next seven days living in trepidation that someone might have reported his actions, knowing that this would then have brought his career to a premature end.

The Tyne & Wear Metro system was initially gated at every station but, following the tragic death of a child who somehow got his head stuck in a barrier at Benton Metro, the decision was made to remove barriers at all but the key central area stations. Even there, they were left to freewheel. The result was that passengers were placed on trust and fares evasion became endemic – until the level of both ticket inspection and prosecution of offenders was increased dramatically to bring it back to more acceptable levels. Ken Livingstone's London bendibuses, which permitted entry by any of their three doors, became widely known as the "free buses" and levels of ticketless travel rose steeply when passengers observed that there would be little chance of detection. Whatever the design of the revenue collection system, it will always be the subject of attack from both employees and customers. Management systems have therefore always been needed

Articulated buses were introduced by London Mayor, Ken Livingstone, in 2002. With entry encouraged through all three doors and high Oyster card usage, low bus stop dwell times were achieved. However, 150 extra ticket checkers had to be employed in a bid to counter their "free bendibus" reputation. This example, seen in Bridge Street, Westminster in October 2011, is a Mercedes 0530G capable of carrying 140 passengers but succeeding Mayor Johnson ensured that they were all gone by December of that year. Operators and vehicle leasing companies were left to dispose of some 380 artics, although replacement double-deck orders provided a boost to UK manufacturers. (Don Akrigg)

Stockport's new bus station was opened in 1981 to accommodate services removed from Mersey Square to make way for the Merseyway Shopping Centre. The GM Buses double-deckers are a MCW Metrobus and four Leyland Atlanteans. The red Leyland National is a Trent vehicle. Originally a North Western (NW) operation, the Buxton service transferred when NW was sold to SELNEC in 1972. Towards the 27-arch viaduct, carrying the London to Manchester main line over the Mersey, stands an ex-NW Alexander DP Bristol RELL6G. Behind that is GM Buses Stockport depot, now owned by Stagecoach Manchester. (Geoffrey Morant)

both to apprehend offenders and to monitor the level of fraud occurring.

Les Burton spent much of his early career working in revenue protection. He started in the North Western traffic office as a teenager and after working as a conductor and driver was first appointed a revenue inspector at the age of 25. He later headed the South Manchester revenue team for GMPTE-owned GM Buses. Checking Inspectors duties also involved ensuring that drivers were not running early and Les reckons that aside from knowing his services, a good inspector needed to be able to appear, by surprise, anywhere on his patch. That was not so easy as it sounded, particularly where frequencies were lower and drivers could work out which bus an inspector would catch next and then signal warnings to colleagues. To overcome this shortcoming, Les would walk considerable distances between routes or use local train services to hop between stations. He told me that on occasions he had even used the Partington-Cadishead ferry across the Manchester ship canal and had been rewarded by catching an unsuspecting Crosville driver who had tampered with his Setright machine. He reckoned that surprise, diligence and an element of luck were often key ingredients to success.

Les's ability to appear where least expected was well known amongst staff and he tells of one instance in the 1970s where he surprised the driver of the last service 330 from Ashton-under-Lyne to Stockport. Having checked a predictable series of other services, Les had caught the train from Rose Hill to Woodley

Stockport Corporation latterly favoured Leyland PD3s. This 1968 example is a 70-seat East Lancs-bodied Leyland PD3/14 in GM Buses colours waiting time at Manchester Piccadilly in September 1980 on the frequent A6 corridor service to Hazel Grove 10 miles away. The driver and conductor appear to prefer their own company to each others. (Geoffrey Morant)

and waited for his 330 bus to arrive. He did not have to wait long as the bus appeared eight minutes early. Les boarded and warned the driver that he would be reported for early running, while he held the bus until the correct departure time. Some 35 years later, in 2011, Les gained responsibility for Fleetwood Depot and on one visit he and a particular driver recognised each other from their Woodley encounter. Before Les could speak, the driver said, "I've told this lot that you will pop up anywhere!"

Les's use of rail services to surprise drivers on one occasion led him to stumble across the Section Inspector's van in a remote station car park. Worse still, he could clearly see his boss, the said Section Inspector, amorously entwined with a lady, whom he also recognised. At this point Les decided that absence of body beat presence of mind and made himself scarce. Some six months later he was summoned to see his District Manager, Fred Kennington. Fred had previously been the Traffic Superintendent of Stockport Corporation and Les reckoned he was one of the best busmen that he had ever worked for. Les feared he was in trouble but

didn't know why when Fred asked him, "How long has it been going on?" On asking what he meant, Fred replied "the relationship between Section Inspector H and Mrs W." Les didn't know how to reply but Fred went further "I am not naive Burton, and neither are you". Les recalls mumbling something about "not long" but shortly afterwards his boss unexpectedly resigned and took his pension. It seemed that Fred would not tolerate any adulterous relationships amongst his staff.

There's no such thing as the "perfect fiddle", although some are more difficult to detect than others and may even require a degree of luck. I was once told of such a deception which, on the face of it, was quite smart. It involved collecting a discarded high-value used ticket from the bus and then upon arrival at the terminus the driver would set up his machine correctly for the next journey. He would then issue the lowest value ticket. He would put the two tickets together and tear them in half. The first unsuspecting passenger to board who asked for the higher value fare would be given two ticket halves. One would show the correct fare and the other would show the correct fare stage, date and ticket number sequence. Perfect? Well yes, until an observant inspector boards and asks the passenger why their ticket is torn in half.

Les Burton also remembers another "perfect fiddle". He was checking one long-serving driver who invariably had his Setright ticket machine date set a couple of days in advance and Les could never fathom out why. On this occasion he had boarded the 192 Service at Chapel Street, Hazel Grove, just one stop from the terminus. Setright ticket machines printed the last three digits of the ticket serial number and when Les checked this vehicle, he found two tickets with the same date and serial number which was impossible. He returned to the office perplexed and then it suddenly dawned on him what the driver was doing. He was issuing tickets with advance dates, and then collecting them from the bus floor or used ticket box when passengers had discarded them. He then re-issued them two days later on the correct date, when the machine was printing ticket numbers in the same sequence, to passengers who were boarding at the same fares stage in locations where he did not expect to be checked. Sweeps of the driver's buses confirmed his deception.

Les recalls another occasion when a chance remark played a big part in catching a thief. He used to play cricket for GM Buses in the PSV league and in the summer of 1984 he was sitting waiting to bat in Bournemouth when he fell into conversation with the then Bournemouth General Manager, Ian Cunningham. Les mentioned that he believed they were employing one of his ex-Bournemouth drivers, Peter W. Ian Cunningham described him to a "T" and then asked Les what job he did. Ian then uttered the fateful words, "Very adept with the TIM machine and a screw-driver." While GM Buses did not use TIMs, they were using Almex A machines and Les knew that it was possible to slide a thin piece of metal into the machine, which could be removed and

replaced at will. Carefully inserted, this had the effect of printing a ticket minus any price information. On returning to Manchester, Les arranged for W's buses to be swept off and, sure enough, many of the tickets he had issued showed no fare paid. It took the best part of twelve months to catch him red-handed, but by that time Les's team had amassed a large amount of evidence against him. Les recalls that W was the only person he was aware of who had been dismissed by GM Buses who also had a lien placed on his pension; hardly surprising given the amount of money he had stolen.

Operators neglect revenue protection and service monitoring at their peril. Ticket machine control is as much a part of this process as observations on the road. When Busways acquired the competing Tyne & Wear Omnibus Company (TWOC) in 1989 we immediately noted that there was no control exercised over the Setright machines used for ticket issue. Drivers could pick up any machine when signing on and there was no record kept of which one they had. A sharp-eyed Busways inspector noted that one particular TWOC driver would alight at Newcastle Central Station with his ticket machine midway through a journey to return some five minutes later. Suspicions aroused, he lay in wait the following day and was surprised to see the

The Tyne & Wear Omnibus Company fleet largely comprised second-hand Bristol LHs. However, this vehicle, standing at Newcastle Central Station was a Leyland PSU4B/4R with Marshall 45-seat body first registered to Maidstone and District. Its registration plate is incorrect and should read EKJ 455K. (Geoffrey Morant)

driver exchanging the ticket machine with another in the left-luggage lockers. By using two machines he was able to ensure that everything was in order whenever an inspector checked his bus but he was also working on a very equitable "one round trip for the Company and one round trip for me" basis.

When Arriva purchased Merseybus in 2000 the competition authorities required it to divest its Gilmoss depot to a third party in order to maintain competition in the area. The Glenvale business had only been created in 2001 by two ex-Merseybus directors to acquire this divestment. It had rapidly expanded including the acquisition of CMT in 2003 but a year later started looking for a buyer. Les Burton recalls that in early 2005 he participated in the due diligence work undertaken before Stagecoach acquired the Glenvale business that summer. He was despatched to Liverpool to take a look at the operations. He began his observations in the café used by the drivers and overheard one driver tell his mates that he was going on holiday tomorrow but "I haven't made a bean yet". Les thought he might be a good place to start, so boarded his bus, a 284

to Southport, and was astonished that not one single passenger, Les included, received a ticket on the whole journey. He returned by train to Liverpool and boarded a service 86 and the driver was again failing to issue tickets to most of those who boarded. When he got to Garston he found five buses parked up and the drivers all playing cards on the front vehicle. It seemed that operating trips as scheduled was optional at Glenvale. This was confirmed for him by another driver whom he observed in Paradise Street bus station reading a book. Les went for a ride to the outer terminus and back on a 75 and when he returned, the bookworm driver was still there. He hadn't moved. As Les commented, it must have been a riveting read.

When Stagecoach acquired the business, Les was appointed Operations Director and in the first twelve months alone over 38% of the drivers either resigned or were dismissed including a group of four drivers who, with the connivance of a member of the depot staff, were booking paid time while playing golf. Les reckons that it took three years of hard work to bring the operations up to Stagecoach standards.

Nearly all of the 1125 Leyland Titan TN15s built, were ordered by London Transport. The first 250 were bodied by Park Royal before Leyland closed that factory in November 1979 and moved production to its Lillyhall facility near Workington. This example entered London service in November 1982. It was sold to Merseybus in 1993 who removed the centre door and up-seated the vehicle to 74. Transferred to Arriva on acquisition, it became part of the Gilmoss depot fleet acquired by Glenvale in 2003. Seen here in July 2005, it sports the name Freda in keeping with Glenvale tradition. (Roy Marshall)

Delivering good customer service is more about attitude than process. The modern tendency for retail staff to conclude transactions with the words "Have a nice day" or, in restaurants, to deliver your food with the parting words "enjoy" fail to impress, particularly when they are uttered mechanically and devoid of any feeling. I recall attending one customer care course at Tyne & Wear PTE where the tutor quickly noted that one long serving colleague was exhibiting negative body language. When asked what his problem was, he told the instructor that he had a lot of work to do that day and he would rather be getting on with it. In any event he had already been on a course where they had "done smiling". Yet it is smiling that makes all the difference, and smiling is a state of mind.

Fifty years ago, the terms "customer service" and "marketing" were rare currency in the bus industry. The customer service function was called "Complaints" and the understanding of marketing went little further than a recognition of the need to advertise. The Bell Punch Company's "Ultimate" ticket machines, with their conductor-issued pre-printed tickets, were then favoured by many municipal operators. Local businesses were encouraged to advertise on the back of the tickets, which could thereby fund the cost of the ticket rolls, but the fall-back advert often starkly read, "Go by Bus". This was a call to action which not only preached to the converted but also risked focussing their attention on the quality of their journey experience and the potential conclusion that they would rather not! As a young manager, I suggested that rather than advertise on the back of bus tickets we should be promoting the benefits of bus travel to motorists on lower rear adverts. I was roundly told that we could make more money if the advertising contractor sold the space to the motor trade.

Typical of industry instructions to platform staff, Midland Red's 1966 Rules & Regulations for Drivers and Conductors included in its introduction the exhortation "courtesy and civility towards others costs nothing and will bring a rich reward in the courtesy and civility received in return." This was as close as it came to asking staff to be nice to passengers. Rule 70 (Attention to Passengers) required conductors to assist children, the elderly and infirm when boarding and alighting; to assist with passengers' luggage and to call out the names

Top: The branding of Trent Barton's ten minute frequency Spondon Flyer service was refreshed and re-launched using four new 37-seat Optare Versas in May 2011. Trent Barton was one of the first to embrace all-over route branding with the assistance of Ray Stenning and his Best Impressions design team. This exploitation of bus-rear advertising is a far cry from the "Go By Bus" advertising of yesteryear. (Ray Stenning)

Centre: More of Ray Stenning's handiwork is evident on this Trent Barton 44-seat Wright-bodied Scania L94 on the Rainbow 4 route captured in 2007. Following motorists are a captive audience and subtly questioning their judgment encourages them to think twice before taking the car next time they travel. (Ray Stenning)

Lower: Good advertising promotes service benefits. Applied to a 45-seat Optare Excel L1180, which was delivered new in 2000, it is seen here in May 2007 marketing Trent Barton's frequent Mickleover-Derby service. (Ray Stenning)

of important points loudly enough to be heard by all passengers. Smiling however was not a specified requirement.

Nothing did more to change management and staff attitudes than the advent of deregulation and privatization. They brought with them an accompanying realization that passengers, or customers as they came to be called, paid the wages and maximized employees' job security. The penny had finally dropped and the more enlightened operators, led by Trent-Barton and some Go Ahead companies, now regularly use bus rears to promote the lifestyle benefits of bus travel.

In the "good old days" there were some employees who just weren't suited to dealing with passengers and in recognition of their obvious shortcomings they were kept away from any customer-facing responsibilities. Sometimes however, such safeguards came unstuck as John Gould now illustrates.

"In the early 1980s, I worked as a detailer/inspector for the West Yorkshire Road Car Co in Bradford. On one particular early Monday morning, I was stationed at

Bradford Interchange and my colleague, Brian Richardson, was at Hammerton Street Depot. It was one of those mornings. Sod's Law prevailed in all of its spite and glory, and everything that could possibly go wrong, duly did. We found ourselves short of buses for service, coaches, drivers and hostesses for the National Express Rapide workings. The early staff bus broke down, there were two shunting accidents in the shed, the night driver had failed to leave a bus parking plan and, to cap it all, the phone system developed a fault, whereby all incoming calls to the building at the Interchange landed on my extension and could not be transferred.

"Due to the constant ringing of the phone, we had to switch communication to walkie-talkie and eventually we got over the numerous crises. At around 8.30 Brian came down to the Interchange to sort out the remaining staffing issues. We had lost some mileage and there was a degree of fall-out in the form of late running. Particularly hard hit was the Bradford to Baildon service, which in any event was often sacrificed in times of resource shortage to enable the company to meet its schools commitments.

"Now between Shipley and Baildon, lived an ex-military retiree, whose pastime it was to sit at his bay window and record any and all bus service aberrations. He would then regularly telephone in to advise us of our shortcomings and generally berate us for what he perceived to be our general unprofessionalism and ineptitude. Well, he had

Upper: Pictured at Bradford Interchange in June 1984 working West Yorkshire Road Car's Bradford-Baildon service, is this 77-seat ECW-bodied Leyland Olympian ONLXB/1R. (Don Akrigg)

Left: Bradford's 1970s bus interchange incorporated a re-modelled Exchange Station. Despite being an award winning structure it was replaced by a new 29-bay saw-tooth conventional bus station which opened in 2001. Today, WYPTE (Metro) provides a free shoppers' service returning passengers to the former on-street terminals. In this 1977 scene are two West Yorkshire Road Car REs, a Leyland National, and a brace of Metro MCW Metrobuses. (Michael Waller)

had a field day this particular morning and immediately upon Brian's arrival in our office the phone rang. Before I could remind him not to pick it up as it would likely be for one of the other occupiers of the building, he did so to be greeted by our irate ex-army colonel who was in full spate.

"Brian was extremely good at his job, particularly on the detailing and man-management side. He was, however, useless when it came to dealing with the public and tended towards a short fuse in times of stress. When I detected, from the patrician tone and volume, that our Colonel was on the phone I feared the worst. However, Brian dealt remarkably well with the situation at first, making all of the right noises in the right places and absorbing the Colonel's indignant and righteous tirade without retort. However, whilst I cannot recall his exact words, he eventually let slip a response that was mildly tainted with sarcasm and which only served to heighten the incandescence of the complainant to a new previously untapped level. The remainder of the exchange took place as follows:

Colonel: 'Young man, do you know who you are talking to?'

Brian: 'No.'

Colonel: 'I am Colonel David Walsingham-Smythe (retired), former county councillor, St Benedict's school governor and Chairman of the Baildon Community Council!'

Brian: 'I see. And do you know who you are talking to?'

Colonel: 'No.'

Brian: 'Good, then f*** off'.

At this, Brian slammed the phone down. The inevitable written complaint arrived to be followed by internal inquires. Due to the switchboard confusion, the call was never attributed to Brian, although I perceived suspicions were high, as his reputation went before him."

While every depot had its Brians, some employees are "customer neutral" until circumstances push them past their trigger point. When conducting in Portsmouth I observed that even the mildest mannered member of platform staff could be driven to abuse his passengers. Like many crew drivers my mate on this occasion had never been a conductor and therefore hadn't received any training on how he should deal with customers. We were working the 1 & 2 service which ran every 12 minutes. This route was one of Portsmouth's famous pan handles, from Paulsgrove to Cosham, then down the main drag through North End to the Guildhall and on to Southsea via Palmerston Road, returning to Cosham via Winter Road and Copnor Road. End to end running time was a tight 70 minutes

Upper: Portsmouth's first 30-footers were delivered in 1959. Reckoned to be the fastest buses in the fleet, these five 64-seat Metro-Cammell-bodied Leyland PD3/6s were re-seated to 70 in 1963 and nicknamed "spaceships" by the staff. Pictured in September 1968 at the Hard terminus of services 148A & B to Leigh Park this vehicle appears to be on a changeover; however, its passengers seem unconcerned. Behind are a 27ft 56-seat Metro-Cammell-bodied Leyland PD2/40 and a 1963 41-seat Weymann bodied Leyland Leopard L1 used for OPO services. (Roy Marshall)

Right: Sporting a revised livery, this 1966 Portsmouth 76-seat Metro Cammell-bodied Leyland PDR1/1 is heading out of town in August 1973. The comprehensive destination display would have been challenging for all but the sharp-sighted. (Geoffrey Morant)

and the approach to the Guildhall was through the main shopping area of Commercial Road, where traffic delays could often be significant.

The 1 & 2 was one of the Corporation's busiest services and the newest buses, front-entrance Leyland Atlanteans, were being progressively allocated to it. It was my experience that you couldn't get round as fast with an Atlantean as you could with an open rear platform Leyland PD2 or 3. This was because many passengers would "hop off" the PDs in slow moving traffic thereby reducing dwell times at the busy stops and, with a good driver, the manual PDs also accelerated faster than the semi-automatic Atlanteans. Given the choice, most staff would have preferred the back loaders, but on this occasion we had been allocated an Atlantean and unfortunately for us, the bus in front was a PD3. We were heavily delayed in Commercial Road and by the time we reached South Parade Pier were six or seven minutes down and beginning to pick up the passengers waiting for the bus behind as well as our own. The northbound leg of the route to Cosham via Copnor was less busy, but the passengers on this section tended to be more demanding of their bus service and on this particular day they certainly demonstrated this to be the case.

A blue-rinse lady boarded at Festing Hotel to tell my driver "You're late!" He said nothing. At the following stop, the same thing happened again, when the first lady to board gave my driver the same hostile "You're late" greeting, and again he held his tongue. At the third stop my driver snapped. Another middle-aged madam boarded and told him he was late, at which he stood up and told her "if you don't like it you can get off and wait for the next one – as it might be on b***** time!" She was shocked at his outburst and no doubt reported him for his sins but I could see that the cumulative impact of the repeated abuse he had received, when he was doing his best to recover the lost time, had finally got to him. This proved to be a valuable lesson for later in my career when I was required to interview platform staff in disciplinary proceedings arising from passenger complaints.

Some staff had a manner and a way with words that enabled them to get away with saying things that might otherwise cause complaint; Gary Nolan recalls one such incident in Rotherham. Canklow Bridge, which carries a railway over the main Brinsworth Road, has an off-centre arch. It had been the subject of many bus bridge strikes and he recalls spending half a day in the driving school practising driving under the bridge with a double-decker. It was

New to Rotherham in 1969, this SYPTE 77-seat Roe bodied Daimler CRG6LX is passing under Canklow bridge. Despite the advised 15ft 6in clearance, there is a nasty intruding arch to snare the unwary. (Gary Nolan)

Given its rural territory, lightweight single-deckers found favour with Highland Omnibuses Limited. This 1969 45-seat Willowbrook-bodied Ford R192 seen here in 1974 at Inverness appears to have few takers for its next journey to Dingwall. (Geoffrey Morant)

more difficult inbound as you had to go well over onto the other side of the road.

Rotherham had this habit of painting upper deck ceilings white on older buses, probably to hide the years of nicotine staining. Brian King was a conductor with a heart of gold and a wicked sense of humour and one Saturday morning he was conducting a Rotherham-bound bus with only one passenger on the top deck – a man in the front seat. The driver misjudged his line and clipped the bridge with the front nearside dome. Brian heard the big bang, went upstairs and found the passenger sitting there covered in white paint flakes like confetti. Brian looked him up and down and said quizzically, "it's a bit early for the wedding in't it?"

Poor customer relations sometimes arise through lack of communication. Colin Bishop tells of his first driving duty on the Isle of Man. The shift went well and his last journey was the four miles back from Port Soderick into Douglas. He waited for his 11pm departure time and when no one appeared set off back to Douglas with an empty bus, and headed for depot. Job well done, he thought. On arrival, he was greeted by an agitated Depot Inspector who told him that he had just received an irate phone call asking why he hadn't brought the passengers back from Port Soderick. Colin explained that there weren't any, to be told that there were twenty of them in the pub, and it was his job to go and get them out! Colin thought, "how was I supposed to know that?"

Some employees became increasingly less helpful to their passengers the longer they did the job. They knew where their bus was going, so why shouldn't their customers? Gordon Hanning recalls observing one such incident not long after his introduction to the world of buses in 1981 in the Highlands of Scotland.

Gordon had been sent out to do some passenger surveys in Dingwall and overheard an exchange between a long-serving driver and a prospective elderly passenger. The lady asked if the bus was going to Strathpeffer, to which the driver replied, "Aye". She went on, "It's just that it says Inverness on the destination board". To which the driver wearily replied in true music hall tradition "And it says India on the tyres, but we're not going there either"

In a similar vein, Brian Souter relates the tale of a lady asking a conductor how long the next bus will be, when she observed that his bus has standing room only. "The same length as this one", he replied. Rising quickly to the challenge she retorted, "And will it also have a monkey swinging from a pole?"

While such behaviour wouldn't be tolerated by any operator nowadays, it is sometimes impossible to please everybody as Gordon Hanning found out when he was working in Norfolk. During his time with Norfolk County Council, he was responsible for the introduction of the distinctively coloured Park & Ride (P&R) buses, which operated from a variety of sites on the radial approaches to Norwich. The livery was green and all the buses left from the same city centre stops, which sometimes resulted in passengers boarding the wrong bus and landing up at a different P&R site.

In an effort to address this problem, and because the number of sites was increasing from four to six, they decided to have six different colours of buses, one for each site. One site had a fleet of rather striking pink buses, which was too much for one homophobic resident who bombarded the Council with complaints about these "gay" buses that he had to watch passing his house every few minutes and which – he made very clear to Gordon and

Not to everyone's taste, this pink liveried 65-seat Wright-bodied VDL DB 250 with matching pink bus shelter accessories, shows Norfolk CC's route branding solution for its Thickthorn Park & Ride service. The bus is owned by Konnectbus of Dereham, which operates twenty-seven services in the Norwich area and was acquired by the Go Ahead Group in March 2010. (John Young)

his colleagues – deeply offended his manhood. It didn't seem to deter the passengers though as there was a marked growth in usage of P&R after the introduction of route branding.

Sometimes platform staff excelled themselves in the way they collectively responded to the public and they often did so without any encouragement from their employers. Today, employees in every depot get spontaneously involved in activities and stunts for numerous charities but in the 1960s such acts of collective social responsibility were less common. I became party to one example of genuine staff kindness of a very different kind during my conducting days in Portsmouth.

I should begin by explaining the Corporation's service numbering system, which was understood by the locals but was something of a mystery to the visitor. Trolleybus routes, which had dwindled to just two by 1963, were numbered. Bus services were lettered, but bus services which had replaced trolley buses were

numbered too. So far so good, but because of the geography of Portsea Island, several services were pan handles and therefore ran over the same sections of road in both directions on both outward and return journeys. To overcome potential passenger confusion, each service therefore had two sequential numbers or letters, e.g. A & B, which later became 1 & 2 etc., one for each direction. Just to add to the potential for confusion, some of the services to the large overspill council estates created in the 1950s used this system, like the A & B and C & D to Paulsgrove, later to become the 1 & 2 and 3 & 4, whereas the 143 and 148A & B services to Leigh Park did not – although, with a nod to the convention, service 143 did manage to use a series of service number suffixes on outbound journeys (143A, B, E and F), with only one service number (143) for inbound journeys.

All six 143 journeys each hour commenced at Ferry Road in Eastney before going via the Dockyard main gates to either Leigh Park (143A and B), Stanley Avenue (143E) or Moneyfield Avenue (143F). On my first occasion conducting the service, I was working the half-hourly 143F journeys to Moneyfield when, as we approached the terminus, the driver slowed down on Martin Road and instructed me to wave at a house on the offside of the road. On reaching the terminus 200 yards further on, he explained that there was a bedridden lady in the house concerned, whose bed had been moved to the downstairs front room, where she could see the passing buses. The Eastney Depot crews were all aware of her condition and on each occasion they passed her house would slow down and give her a wave. As we set off from the terminus, my driver slowed again on Martin Road, opened the doors and we both gave her a cheery wave. She later wrote to the local paper, The Portsmouth Evening News, thanking the busmen for their kindness and adding that Christmas Day was for her the worst day of the year, as there were no buses running and therefore no waves from the bus crews.

One customer service matter which has been regulated since 1934, and remains so to this day with minor alterations, has been the procedure for dealing with Lost Property – or more properly found property. The regulations require platform staff to search vehicles at every terminus for lost property and for passengers to hand it to them. It must then be retained by the Company for a period and a fee may be charged if the item is reclaimed. Further rules govern the disposal of unclaimed property. Stories abound of unusual items being handed in as well as the staple diet of the lost property trade: umbrellas, scarves and gloves, etc.

Ian Manning told me of one such unusual case, which occurred when Bill Lewis was General Manager of Southampton City

Transport. It related to a set of false teeth which had been handed in by a conductor when they had been found by a passenger on his bus. An old man duly came to the Lost Property Office to enquire whether his teeth had been found on a Number 7 bus the previous day. The clerk checked the Lost Property Register and duly found the said dentures. They were placed on the counter and the man fitted them in his mouth, filled in the paperwork and left, thanking the clerk profusely for reuniting him with his gnashers. He returned the following day, removed them from his mouth, placed them on the counter and then exclaimed indignantly, "They're not mine!"

Nowadays, operators are increasingly at risk from the compensation culture which bedevils contemporary Britain. In these circumstances the customer is not "always right", as the modern customer relations handbook might suggest. It is regrettable that an increasing number of people are prepared to "try it on" if they think the operator might pay out. The following example of an email which was received by Mark Fowles in April 2012, well illustrates the problem which companies now frequently face. It read as follows:

This 1967 AEC Regent V was one of ten delivered to Southampton City Transport in 1967 with Neepsend 74-seat bodywork. In 1964 Cravens acquired East Lancs Coachbuilders and, to increase production capacity, set up the Neepsend plant in Sheffield which built buses to East Lancs specifications until 1968. (Roy Marshall)

"I was recently in the centre of the city of Nottingham enjoying my day out and appreciating the weather. However, my day took a turn for the worse at around 2.30 in the afternoon and I'm afraid to say one of your buses played a key role in the upset that occurred. To set the scene for you, I had just come out of the cinema after watching Titanic 3D on my own, so I was already upset and jittery. I decided to grab something to eat from Subway, so I purchased a 6in Meatball marinara with lettuce and sweetcorn and a cup of Diet Coke to enjoy and wash down the meatball goodness. Yummy! HOWEVER, as I was walking through the city to approach a wonderful place to sit down, eat my sandwich and drown out the sorrows of the Titanic I had just witnessed in three dimensions, disaster struck.

"As I walked past one of your 'Brown Line' buses, the air-brakes suddenly released air near me and startled me to such an extent that I dropped the cup of my beverage to the floor causing all of its contents to spill over the pavement. I sadly had to endure an afternoon where my thirst was not quenched after my Meatball Marinara sandwich (which was very salty but don't worry, Subway will also be receiving an e-mail of complaint), as I did not have the funding to purchase another drink. What's worse is the pure embarrassment I suffered when the event happened. Children laughed at me and people looked at me in a way that broke me.....feeling worthless. I had to flee the scene. It then hit me that I risked being apprehended for littering in our beautiful city.... but I didn't have the courage to return to the scene.

"You were once my favourite bus company but now I feel our relationship is on the edge. I'm writing to you to see how you will react to regain the trust of a once loyal customer.

"Looking forward to hearing from you"

Perhaps the moral of all of these tales is that good customer service is often more easily promised than delivered and that some customers can never be satisfied. Nevertheless, unlike their predecessors, today operators recognize that they need to put constant effort into securing their customers' loyalty.

Nottingham City Transport has now implemented colour coded route branding. This Optare Solo SR, dedicated to its Hucknall Road Brown Line services, is seen in August 2012 pausing for a pedestrian striding purposefully across its bows. (Nottingham City Transport)

FROM THE UNION OFFICE

No canter round the bus industry would be complete without a trade union view, particularly when most large bus operators recognize, and always have recognized, trade unions. The predominant platform staff trade union was the Transport & General Workers (TGWU), now Unite, but in some areas it was (and is) the National Union of Railwaymen (NUR), or the General, Municipal and Boilermakers Union (GMB) to which the employees belonged. Douglas Bailey MBE, kindly agreed to let me interview him in order to get his take, from a trade union perspective, on the way the industry has changed over the years. Douglas came into the business as a twenty-one year old in his home town of Bolton. Having wanted to be a bus driver from the age of twelve, he waited until the day after his twenty-first birthday (In those days, the minimum age for gaining a PSV driving licence was 21) before approaching the Corporation to see whether he could get a bus driving job. Unusually, Bolton was one of those undertakings which was prepared to recruit drivers straight to the cab, without first having served an apprenticeship on the platform as a conductor. Douglas told it like this.

"It was Monday November 6th 1961 and I made an appointment to go down to the transport offices where I had a short interview with the Traffic Superintendent who sent me to see the Senior Driving Inspector, John Sutton. John was a formidable man. He walked me through the garage at Shifnall Street, which

was the first time I had not sneaked in, and over to a Craven-bodied Crossley which was the driver training vehicle. It hadn't been modified in any way, other than by the removal of the window between the driver's cab and the saloon. We went on a twenty minute test drive and then John Sutton told me 'You've not done so bad, Douglas, but you are only twenty-one and used to driving a small van. You'll have to be twenty-three before I can consider you.' This was normal practice for most Lancashire operators at that time. It was probably the first time in my life when I decided I had got to say something. I told him that I had been waiting to become a bus driver ever since I was twelve. I have a job now but I really want to be a bus driver. He said, 'Douglas, it's against my better judgment, but I know that you really mean that. Go and tell them that you've passed'.

"I remember my first duty which was as a 5am standby. I was given duty F1 on the 43 service to Farnworth Black Horse with Edith Nelson as my conductress, who taught me one unwritten rule on that very first journey in service. We left the terminus on Great Moor Street when she gave me the starting signal. The first set of lights was on red and a man

Untreated snow can play havoc with bus schedules, particularly when roads are blocked by other vehicles struggling to gain traction but the driver of this manual gearbox Bolton Corporation 1961 73-seat East Lancs-bodied Leyland PD3/4 appears to be making steady progress in the winter of 1967. Transferred to SELNEC PTE in November 1969, the bus was sold to Squirrels Coaches in Suffolk in 1974. (Photobus)

came running over to the bus. I opened the doors and let him board and then turned right to continue the journey. I think he was our only passenger. We reached the terminus at Farnworth and I jumped out of the cab, proud to have completed my first trip. I boarded the bus and sat down with my conductress who I had never met before. She asked me my name and then she said 'Douglas, let me just tell you something. Never, ever do that again'. Confused, I said, 'Do what?' She continued 'You don't do that. No runners. We were late and he had missed it anyway. If we had been on time he wouldn't have even seen the bus'.

A couple of weeks later I was sat in the canteen and an old driver came up to me and said 'What made you come here? Could you not find something better?' I said 'Certainly not, I've been waiting to be a bus driver'. He said 'I'll give you a tip. The hardest thing about being a bus driver is getting here. Once you are here it's the easiest job in the world'.

"The family then moved to Blackpool in 1964 but there was no work available at the Corporation so I went to Ribble in Preston and after the obligatory Company driving test, was appointed as a driver. All new drivers were assigned to the Corporation rota, which comprised town services operated jointly with the Corporation. It was the hardest work in the depot, and because of the seniority system the longer serving drivers worked the easier longer distance services. What I thought was particularly unfair was that the Corporation drivers earned more than we did for doing the same work. I recognized that to try and change this would be futile, particularly as 80% of the Ribble Preston staff had already done their time on the Corporation rota and my suggestion to mix up the work was firmly rejected by the union officials. The daily travelling was not easy and in 1965 I applied to Lytham St Anne's Corporation, who insisted that all new recruits should conduct before they could go driving. As with my previous jobs I joined the trade union. There were 100% union agreements in place throughout the industry and it was part of the employment contract that union membership was obligatory. I supported that because I believed that everyone benefited from

Until deregulation, Ribble ran a number of joint services with Preston Corporation. Seen leaving Preston Bus Station is this 1955 61-seat Metro-Cammell-bodied Leyland PD2/12 on a wet day in 1970. (Geoffrey Morant)

Ribble took delivery of fifty-nine 49-seat Leyland National Series 1s in 1976. This example, in a replica pre-nationalization livery, is seen at Bolton in 1987 as a passenger boards for Chorley, with a GM Buses Northern Counties-bodied Leyland Atlantean behind it. (Omnibus Society collection - Peter Henson)

This 1957 Lytham St Annes 63-seat MCCW-bodied Leyland PD2/21 has a full standing load as it approaches Squires Gate Lane in August 1970. Lytham became Fylde Borough Council in 1974 and the arms-length company formed at deregulation was sold in December 1993, only for the new owners to sell to neighbouring Blackpool Transport Services in July 1996. (Roy Marshall)

the union's endeavours and should contribute to the funds. I didn't enjoy conducting particularly because I really wanted to be in the cab. One Saturday I was conducting a service 11A from Lytham into Blackpool. We had a full load and I was upstairs collecting fares when we stopped outside Squires Gate bus depot. Two refined ladies were getting off and shouted up, 'Conductor, you've not got our fares'. I shouted down 'I'll see you next time'.

"When I reported for work on the Monday, I was told to go and see Ronald Armstrong, General Manager. I knocked and was told to enter. He said, 'I've had a report that two ladies offered to pay their fares on your bus and you said you would see them next time. You will be pleased to know that they immediately came into the depot and paid their fares so we have their money. All I'm going to say to you is this: if you want to give free rides, that's fine but you will pay for them out of your own pocket'. That's a lesson I have never forgotten.

"Family circumstances caused me to move again and in 1966 I applied to join J. Fishwick and Son at Golden Hill, Leyland. The company, which still operates today, ran services mainly between Leyland and Preston and which in those days were jointly operated with Ribble. I took the company driving test which I passed. When I first signed on I was told that there was a drinks machine in the garage – that was the canteen! It was a complete culture shock. When the cry went out, 'Bus starting', everyone vacated the garage to avoid the inevitable choking exhaust fumes. The union secretary left and I thought to myself things could be better than this, so I stood for, and was elected, the Union secretary. I could take you to Golden Hill now and show you a building, which I had a large part in delivering. There were no facilities at the Preston end either, so I asked the management to provide us with a proper canteen. It was a struggle but eventually we got a room for our drinks machine. I knew that it would be difficult to get things done at Fishwick's and I left to join the railways.

"My time at BR as a guard lasted just six weeks. One engine driver told me that he belonged not to a trade union, but to an association: ASLEF. He said 'We are at the front and you are at the back. Even if you have to get into the engine – you get in the back and

Leyland built five prototype Titan B15s with Gardner engines, two of which went to London Transport. First registered in 1975 by Leyland Bus, this 71-seater was the fourth built and one of three eventually bought by J Fishwick & Sons. (Geoffrey Morant)

we get in the front. It's even better if we have a long rake of wagons because then, we are at the front and you are right at the back'. These divisions weren't for me and I decided that I would try to go back to Fishwick's. I heard on the grapevine that a driver had left so I rang the manager John Brindle, who was the grandson of the original founder, to be told that he had no vacancies. I said are you sure and he said, 'Yes, Douglas, there are no vacancies'.

"So, on 22nd November 1969, I approached Ribble at their Chorley depot. Chorley, with about sixty buses, was a smaller depot than Preston and was friendlier. People would sooner work at Chorley than at Preston. No one even approached me to join the T & G and I had to ask to join. For the first three years I was just an ordinary union member. My first taste of strikes was in 1970 when the company implemented a Monday to Friday working week with weekends covered by overtime. The transition to the new arrangement was botched. Some depots were workings at weekends and some were not. The deal was negotiated centrally but some delegates' reports back were distorted and led to strikes at their depots. This led to a strike at Chorley too, while others went back to work. The whole thing was a mess, with picket lines all over the place and all because of poor communications. However, once the issues were resolved, the Monday to Friday agreement endured from 1971 to 1992.

"The principle of trade unionism is, in my opinion, great but unfortunately governments have interfered and I wish they hadn't, because they have taken authority away from the union officials. Negotiations used to take place with delegates and they would eventually come to an agreement. That can't happen today, because pay awards usually have to be put to the workforce in a ballot. I believe that the record would show that nowadays workforce first ballots reject the offer from the employer and talks have to begin again. Trade unions are averse to recommending things any more because if they do the workforce vote against it. It's almost as though they are suspicious of the trade unions' endeavours on their behalf. It used to be that when trade union officials made decisions on behalf of the workforce, the workforce could vote them out at the next trade union election, in much the same way that we vote at elections to keep, or to change, a government in the country.

"I was elected to the Chorley Branch Union Committee in 1971 and became Branch Secretary in 1972 when the previous Secretary retired. I believe that over the following twenty years the trade union was able to get the best employees' terms and conditions of employment possible, through some difficult times. In 1989 we became part of Stagecoach. I am of the view that Stagecoach is one of the better major bus groups. The company works with you and recognizes there is a role for the trade union, but they were, and remain, hard taskmasters. If you give Stagecoach a reasonable case you will get a reasonable response. We asked for, and got, a national consultative structure, one of the first in the post-deregulation bus industry. I was one of its founder members and I was proud to play a part in the Stagecoach national Cab Design Committee which helped design the cab in the Alexander Enviro 400. I was also a member of the TGWU National Passenger Trade Group Committee and was its chairman from 2000 to 2005."

I asked Douglas what he thought made a good manager. He told me that, in his view, a good manager requires honesty, the ability to listen as well as to speak, and recognition that he or she is dealing with human beings. Nine out of ten managers recognise that. Put simply, a bad manager is one who doesn't know what he (or she) is doing. He said he wouldn't tolerate that and would make representations to have them replaced because it was bad for the business, and therefore ultimately bad for the employees that he represented.

At the age of 71, Douglas still drives one day a week for Stagecoach in his home town of Chorley.

Post-deregulation, many operators introduced urban minibus networks. With lower wages, cheaper capital costs and better penetration of residential areas, the economics seemed attractive. Pictured alongside Chorley bus station in 1994, this 25-seat Alexander Sprint-bodied Mercedes 709D is operating on Stagecoach's town service network. The Zippy branding looks to be something of an afterthought. (Roy Marshall)

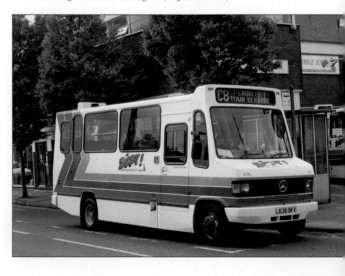

WHO'S IN CHARGE?

Shop floor militancy increased through the 1960s and 70s and was often called the "British Disease." It afflicted the bus industry like many others. The number of unofficial stoppages varied from operator to operator and from garage to garage but the larger operators in the big cities usually suffered the most. Legislation to prevent secondary picketing and to require workforce ballots before strike action helped to reduce these conflicts but it was only the advent of deregulation in the bus industry that brought the beginning of an end to many Spanish customs.

To begin turning things round it was often necessary to get the staff to understand that rules matter. A good place to start was with the proper wearing of the uniform supplied by the operator, since this sent a clear message to all that the place was "under new management" and it also looks so much more professional out on the road. In 1994, Les Burton was sent to Queen's Road depot in north Manchester. It should have been one of GM Buses top performing depots but things had begun to drift. Les noted that many drivers were coming to work in non-uniform shirts and advised the trade union that this was going to stop. A Staff Notice was displayed which made it clear that incorrect uniform would mean the employee being sent home to change – with consequent lost payment. "U" day came and the first driver to report without a uniform shirt at 4.34am was sent home. As soon as the trade union secretary came in he asked to see Les. Les made clear that he wasn't for changing and went further by

saying that he personally would wear a white shirt (which was the colour of the then GM Buses uniform shirt) every day himself and he expected all the drivers to do the same. So for the next two years Les wore a white shirt and with it any bus company tie he could blag from around the country!

It was not only the big cities where these management issues arose. There were other places where the business appeared to be run for the benefit of the employees and not the passengers who were paying their wages. One such example was Glossop. The ex-mill town nestling at the foot of the Pennines, Glossop had sported a bus garage since the early days of North Western. Geographically it was the end of the Empire and had never received the management attention it deserved throughout its entire existence. As a consequence, the drivers there pretty much ran the place. Once North Western became part first of SELNEC and then GM Buses it was still out on a limb. The situation deteriorated when it became managed jointly with Ashton. This meant that senior drivers who lived in the nearby Hattersley estates could seek a transfer to Glossop. This had attractions for them, as by then they were being paid the same rates of pay as Manchester but Glossop local services were considerably easier work than either their Tameside or Manchester equivalents. Drivers did pretty much as they pleased, including telling old ladies that the 2.45pm journey wouldn't be running that afternoon because of anticipated problems with the bus; this was

Manchester's Queens Road depot was first opened for trams in 1901 and is now Grade II listed. Today owned by First Manchester, its top sheds house the Greater Manchester Museum of Transport. Accessed from Boyle Street, which was named after the Councillor who laid its foundation stone, the place still has a tram depot feel to it. GM Buses continued the Manchester Corporation policy of vehicle standardization and these buses are all Leyland Atlanteans with bodywork by Wigan-based, Northern Counties. (Ronald Barton)

Above: Glossop, where the drivers "pretty much ran the place". The former Stockport Leyland on the joint service number 6 to Manchester stands outside the Norfolk Arms where the very first North Western buses to be based in the town were garaged in the 1920s. On the corner, one of SHMD's short Daimler Fleetlines stands ready to move off on a local service while just visible is a North Western single-decker on the Buxton service. The main A57 road to Sheffield, and where Les Burton found a bus casually left with its engine running, is to the photographer's left. (John Senior)

Right: The depot, a typical BET-designed construction, is seen with part of its allocation of AEC Renowns and two Willowbrook-bodied Leyland Tiger Cub single-deckers. North Western operated no highbridge vehicles, though near the end of its life former Leyland Titans from Ribble were drafted in for driver training purposes. Stagecoach moved the Glossop fleet to new premises in Ashton under Lyne in 2009. (Photobus)

code for the driver will be watching football on the television in the pub.

Stagecoach acquired GM Buses (South) in 1996 and with it Les Burton, who was appointed to run the Hyde Road and Glossop depots. Les tells of his first visit to Glossop in his new role. When he arrived at the garage one of the drivers, I'll call him John Smith, was washing his car. Les told him that he should not be doing this in paid time to which the driver replied, "We do what we want here. You managers come and go". Les asked him how much service he had and Smith replied "29 years", to which Les retorted "You won't see 30, if you don't mend your ways. Now put that hose away and shift your car out of the garage".

A few weeks later, Les was again visiting Glossop when he saw a Metrobus parked on the pavement with its engine running while the driver was in the pie shop. Les got into the cab and drove the bus back to depot, to be followed some time later by driver Smith who had caught the next bus back. Smith was decidedly unhappy and was even more so when

the Depot Manager gave him a written warning for his sins, against which he immediately lodged an appeal. When Les went to Glossop to hear the appeal, driver John said "What's he doing here?" and it was explained to him that Les would hear appeals against the Depot Manager's decisions. John said "It's no use appealing to him. He won't overrule it" and promptly withdrew his appeal.

Six months after their first encounter, Les was in Ashton Bus Station when a lady came up to him to complain that she had missed the service 238 bus, which ran from Glossop to Tameside Hospital, and that it had been 13 minutes early. The driver was contacted on the radio and when asked where he was stated that he was "Just coming through Dukinfield". The lady was adamant that the bus had already been and gone so Les went into the PTE Offices upstairs where there would be CCTV footage of the bus station. It did not take long to establish that the lady was indeed right. Subsequent enquiries revealed that the driver had been none other than John Smith. Following his

All seems quiet enough in Ashton's bus station but the early departure of the 238 service to Tameside Hospital was to have severe repercussions for its driver. (John Senior)

dismissal, he went to an employment tribunal and lost – with the tribunal unusually announcing its decision at the end of the hearing and making him pay his own costs. In consequence, he never reached his 30 years service. Les said that Glossop was the sort of place where if you kicked one of them, they would all bruise, but his firm actions provided the impetus needed to re-establish a good bus service in the town.

Les also recalls some four years later being instructed to spend a couple of weeks managing operations at the principal depot of another Stagecoach subsidiary, where performance was falling below expectations. I'll not say which, in order to spare the blushes of some who were responsible for the unit and are still working elsewhere in the industry today. Les knew that he wasn't going to be there for long so he decided that he had to make an example of the right people, as soon as the opportunity arose – as he knew it surely would.

The Manager was away at a meeting and Les was in the depot when the trade union secretary had refused to take a Volvo B10M for his duty. It is a standard rule throughout the industry that provided a bus is roadworthy, drivers should take the buses which they have been allocated. Les ensured that the driver understood that he would be suspended if he persisted with his refusal, which he did, and so he was. The full time union officer was notified and an hour later was on the phone to Les. 'The

secretary tells me that you are a t***", he told Les. 'That's right, I am,' Les replied, 'Why don't you come in for a cup of tea, and you can judge for yourself".

The following morning they met for their cuppa and Les explained that the trade union secretary was likely to be awarded a final warning and three days suspension, which would be increased by a day on each occasion he challenged it during interview. The interview took place and as it progressed the secretary complained, 'It's not right this!' The full time officer advised his colleague that he should make no adverse comment as it might prove costly for him. Again the secretary said 'I don't think this is right', at which the full time officer told him to shut up. Les then explained that the purpose of the disciplinary procedure was not just to punish but also to correct. He asked the trade union secretary what he would do in future if he was allocated a B10M. The secretary gritted his teeth and then mumbled, 'I will take the f****** thing.' Les pretended he couldn't hear and asked the secretary to repeat his confirmation. 'I'll take it.' he said. Following a short adjournment Les announced his decision, which was a final warning and five days suspension.

Les told me that the interesting thing about this whole episode was that it had been triggered by a worried telephone call from the trade union chairman to senior Stagecoach management to the effect that the place was rapidly going downhill and could they come and do something about it.

In the 1990s, Stagecoach standardized on the Alexander PS-bodied Volvo B10M for single-deck orders, notwithstanding reservations from at least one of Les Burton's UK union officials! This vehicle was one of five air-conditioned 51-seat examples delivered to its Hong Kong operations in 1994 and transferred to Wellington, New Zealand, in 1996. The overhead wires powered the seventy trolleybuses, which were also acquired when Wellington City Transport was privatized in 1992. Stagecoach sold its New Zealand transport interests to Infratil in 2005. (Tony Hall)

TAKE ME TO THE METROCENTRE

The Metrocentre was the UK's first out of town retail Mecca. In 1981 the Tyneside Enterprise zone was created and, seizing the opportunity presented, Ashington miner's son John Hall concluded that the Geordies were ready for a US style shopping mall. The site was a boggy, derelict power station wasteland on the south bank of the river Tyne in western Gateshead. A railway ran through it but there was no station. The site was also bounded by the A1 and the river Tyne. The nearest river crossings were at Scotswood, two miles to the west and at Redheugh, two miles to the east. This was hardly the ideal location for what was to become a 1.8 million square feet shopping and leisure destination, but Hall and his developers had calculated that with a new access to the A1 Western bypass, 1.5 million people lived within a thirty minute drive time and that would make the development viable.

I first became involved with the developers in 1984 when, as Traffic Manager of Tyne & Wear PTE, I was roundly told that bus services were no part of their access plans. The Passenger Transport Authority was ambivalent towards the development as its members could see that it would suck trade out of the existing centres which they represented and so there the matter rested until immediately after the first mall opened for trade on 14th October 1986. As Commercial Director of the newly created Busways Company, I received a phone call from none other than John Hall himself, asking whether we could provide a bus service to his new development as further phases would be opening shortly before Christmas. A fortnight later at the face-to-face meeting it transpired that not only had the retailers in the first phase received requests from shoppers for bus services but they were also having difficulty recruiting retail staff, many of whom needed buses to get to work. After Hall had explained his problem, I politely pointed out that I had been trying to engage his people about the provision of buses for over two years and in any event he had left it too late as he couldn't have any buses before 26th January 1987! This was because after deregulation day on 26th October 1986 there was a moratorium on further service changes for a three month period.

Hall was incredulous, but I was also aware that the Metrocentre represented an important commercial opportunity for Busways,

particularly when the location was in Go Ahead Northern Company's territory and they too might want to operate from Newcastle to the site. So we struck a deal, if Hall could persuade Ministers to give us a dispensation from the new regulation, we would be up and running before Christmas 1986.

Before driving back to Newcastle Keith Moffatt, my Commercial Officer, and I toured the site and quickly realised that it was going to become a major traffic generator. We planned our new service and quickly concluded that it needed to be a non-stop express operation calling at three Newcastle city centre stops to provide convenient interchange with cross-city bus services, the Metro at Monument, and national rail services at Central Station. We also picked a memorable number, 100, thereby breaching the carefully planned area-based service numbering system we had introduced jointly with Northern and United some ten years earlier and which extended from the Scottish Borders to Teesside and North Yorkshire. The Metrocentre shuttle was thus launched in early December 1986, initially as a fifteen minute frequency minibus service.

Reaction was mixed. Go Ahead were huffy because we had beaten them to it; Newcastle City Council was incensed because we were terminating in Blackett Street, the heart of the city shopping core and the PTE was compromised by the PTA's ambivalence, so sat on its hands. Danny Marshall, the Chairman of the PTA, Busways then-owners, was a prominent Newcastle councillor whose ward was in the west end of the city. I agreed with him that Service 7 would be extended from Scotswood Bridge to the Metrocentre, as soon as legislation permitted in 1987, and he would keep his city council colleagues in order and stop them pursuing plans to evict buses from Blackett Street – a bargain which we both were to keep.

Most importantly, passengers took to the service like ducks to water and in next to no time we had to run larger single-deck vehicles. In those early days the only direct route into the Metrocentre from the Redheugh Bridge involved using Cross Lane with its 13ft 9in railway bridge. With a fleet of highbridge double-deckers, instructions were issued that double-deck duplicates must always run via the longer Scotswood Bridge route to access the development from the west end.

Not long after, Keith Moffatt applied for, and was appointed to, the newly created post of Divisional General Manager for the Gateshead operations of the Go Ahead Northern Company. It took him less than three months to launch the son of service 100 – the X66 service from Gateshead Metro to the Metrocentre!

Patronage on the Metrocentre shuttle continued to grow and in 1990 the Western by-pass slip roads were opened providing another route from the east into the site. However, the complex was becoming a victim of its own success and traffic queues on the by-pass at busy shopping times became a regular feature, so service 100 continued to use the "back door" via Cross Lane, as did Go Ahead Northern's service X66. And of course the inevitable happened. In the space of thirty months no fewer than five double-deckers came to grief under the railway bridge. Because of the bridge height there were fortunately no passenger injuries, but the damage was sufficiently spectacular to attract media attention on each occasion. Northern, who led the battle honours 3-2 were called before the Traffic Commissioner to explain why their Operator's licence shouldn't be revoked and after our second bridge strike I held a detailed inquiry to establish how it had happened, with the objective of ensuring that it would never happen again.

I interviewed everyone involved on that fateful day including, much to the consternation of their trade unions, the engineering staff on duty. It seemed that on this occasion the driver, who was a regular on the Metrocentre rota, had asked for a changeover because he had a defect on his allocated single-decker. The engineers had no single-deckers available and gave him a double-deck in exchange. While they advised control of the change, control had failed to remind the driver to use the alternative Scotswood Road route, although he had done so on the outward journey. However, on the return, as he departed the Metrocentre bus station he turned right instead of left and followed the single-deck route for a couple of hundred metres where he proceeded without further thought under the notorious Cross Lane bridge. Here was a long serving driver with an excellent disciplinary and accident record, who went the way he always went but had forgotten he was driving a double-decker. Just how many times has that explanation been given, before and since, by drivers who have committed bridge strikes?

The resulting instruction to staff was more draconian than its predecessor, and it was this.

At just 13ft 9in (4.12m) clearance here is seven to nine inches (18-23cm) short of the typical highbridge double-deck configuration as Busways and Northern can testify, Cross Lane Bridge, near Gateshead Metrocentre, will remove the roof, shatter the top-deck windows and leave seated passengers shocked but otherwise uninjured. (Peter Nash)

Under no circumstances were double-deckers to be allocated to services operating to the Metrocentre, and any manager, engineer or inspector who did so could expect to be found guilty of gross misconduct.

That certainly put a stop to the decapitations and since then a new local highway network has been put in place around the Metrocentre, including a new bridge over the railway, making the use of Cross Lane unnecessary. I understand, however, that the "no double-deckers" instruction remains in place at Stagecoach in Newcastle to this day.

Below: Not just a shuttle, but a super-shuttle, this new 49-seat Optare Delta-bodied DAF SB 220 leaves Gateshead Metrocentre in 1990 for its non-stop run to Gateshead Metro Interchange. (Roy Marshall)

Foot: In 1994, Busways purchased this 51-seat Optare Sigma bodied-Dennis Lance for evaluation. It is seen here in August 1995 in Market Street, Newcastle, operating the Metrocentre Shuttle. Busways was by then part of Stagecoach as evidenced by the nearside windscreen cube and the revised strap line beneath the nearside logo. The double-deckers are Alexander-bodied Leyland Atlantean AN68s inherited with the Tyne & Wear PTE fleet in 1986. (Mark Watson)

THAT'S PREPOSTEROUS!

Deregulation had been underway less than a year when competition came to the North East big style in the shape of the Tyne & Wear Omnibus Company (TWOC). TWOC was the brain child of Bob Lewis, the proprietor of Trimdon Motor Services Limited, who also had extensive business interests in Jersey, including the island's sole bus operator, Jersey Motor Transport. The TWOC operation relied largely on second-hand Bristol LH single-deckers and targeted the Busways networks in Newcastle and later Sunderland too. It was eventually purchased by Go Ahead Northern in 1989 and sold on to Busways on the same day.

In 1991 competition resurfaced, this time led by Harry Stewart who had been a traffic supervisor at TWOC. He had enlisted the assistance of the partners in a Gateshead Haulage Company, CPS, and this time a fleet of brand new Metrorider minibuses was deployed. Harry was an ex-PTE employee and the rumour mill shortly before the Company launched worked overtime with stories about a decisive marketing initiative that the new operator was about to deploy. On the first day of Welcome Passenger Services operation this decisive marketing initiative became abundantly apparent. Welcome had not only copied Busways routes and service numbers but had also adopted the Busways livery, the only distinguishing feature being the Welcome fleet-name on the vehicles.

Immediately, I phoned our lawyers in Leeds to be put through to their intellectual property expert, Richard Boardman. Richard was a likeable fellow with a sharp legal mind and a track record in intellectual property litigation, particularly in the fashion industry where legal remedies were apparently quite common. Richard loved to negotiate and I was told how, when his wife went into labour with their first child, Richard was in attendance in the delivery suite. As the birth approached, the doctors had offered his wife a pain-killing drug, which she readily agreed to, but when it came to sign the standard disclaimer, Richard insisted on revising some of the legalese at the foot of the document. You can imagine the scene: Richard taking out his pen and saying "it will be all right if we just make this small change", his wife screaming for the injection, and the junior doctor torn between administering the medicine and wondering how to handle a lawyer who

had the temerity to seek to re-write the standard NHS disclaimer. I am not sure how the situation was resolved but mother and baby both did well.

Once he had seen the evidence, Richard was sure that we had a case for "passing off" and a letter before action was immediately sent to Welcome demanding they re-livery their buses and stop using the Busways service numbers. There was no response from Welcome and so on Richard's advice we sought an injunction at the High Court in London where, in Richard's view, there were QC's and judges well-used to dealing with cases of passing off. I had not previously understood the significance of the injunction process, which is there to prevent somebody continuing with a particular course of action on the basis that there may possibly have been a breach of the plaintiff's rights. If the injunction is granted then the substantive case as to whether or not there actually was a breach would be heard many months later, at which point the loser would not only be liable for very substantial legal costs but also for the loss of business occasioned to the other from the date the injunction was first granted. In other words, the parties would be playing for very big stakes, which is why most cases of this nature never get beyond the injunction stage, and why most injunctions are not contested.

Welcome, to our amazement, decided to contest the injunction and it was duly listed for a three day hearing at the High Court in London. When briefing our QC it was clear that we had a good case for the copying of our livery and he was intrigued by the concept of property in route numbers, which he found "interesting." This raised alarm bells with me since in my experience lawyers who find things "interesting" also expect you to fund their making legal history in test cases.

The first day of the hearing arrived and in introducing the case our QC had to explain the concept of bus deregulation to the judge. He described how, outside London, any bus operator who held an operator's licence could, with 42 days notice, register a bus service to run anywhere they wished. At this point the judge intervened, "Did you say, anywhere?" he asked incredulously. Our QC turned round for confirmation and I nodded my head. "Yes, I am advised anywhere, my Lud" he replied. The judge paused for a second or two to digest what he had heard and then said, "Well that's preposterous".

So here we were nearly five years into deregulation and the judge, who must have lived his entire life within the M25, hadn't got a clue what it was all about. But, give the man his due, he did at least find in favour of our injunction. Welcome saw sense at last and the matter didn't go any further in the courts, so we never found out whether or not there could be property in route numbers.

Below: Welcome began trading in Newcastle with ten new 29-seat Optare Metroriders and seven new 28-seat Reeve Burgess-bodied Renault S75s in October 1991. Pictured on Blackett Street two weeks later, this Metrorider has gained two additional vinyl blue stripes and a 400 (rather than 40) service number in an early reaction to Busways litigation. (David Clark)

Foot: Pictured in April 1993, this Welcome Renault S 75 has been repainted to become a predominantly red bus following Busways' successful High Court action to prevent Welcome "passing off" its livery. It is also displaying revised service number 380, following a route which mirrors Busways 38 service. (Geoffrey Morant)

DESTINATION DISPLAYS

Since the days of the first motor buses, operators have advertised the ultimate destination of their vehicles by fixing destination boards to the front and sides. As networks grew, they added service numbers and eventually upgraded to linen destination blinds. These were usually printed black on white linen, so that the unpainted numerals and text could be seen at night when back illuminated. It soon became common practice to display both route number and ultimate destination with a separate via blind to the front with optional side and rear blinds as well.

Some operators gave more information than others and not all platform staff shared their employer's enthusiasm to assist intending passengers. If Inspectors were not on top of them, the destinations displayed could soon be reduced to the bare minimum. Taffy Evans would have turned in his grave if he had seen some of United's buses in the 1970s displaying just a service number and the word "Service" or "United". Other operators, like OK Motor Services, didn't believe in service numbers at all, despite running a network of services and instead relied solely on the use of an ultimate destination alongside the painted letters "OK".

Depending upon which part of the country you were in, duplicates carried either the words "Relief", "Extra", or "Duplicate." Buses running out of service before deregulation tended to display "Private", or "Special", which was code for "Not you" or else nothing at all. This changed with deregulation when the more

friendly words "Sorry not in Service" started to appear in its place. In Newcastle, a few PTE drivers discovered that the additional letters E, S and X on the numeral blinds could be used to display the word SEX, which they seemed to think was hilariously funny. In the Manchester area, buses which were running part route displayed an X after the number, and in the 1950s and 60s before the Clean Air Acts, when winter smog could be a real problem, the via blind was replaced by the word "FOG" – meaning that the bus would go as far as it could – to wherever that might be.

The advent of one-person operation meant that drivers were understandably reluctant to leave their cash unattended in the cab so, increasingly, buses only displayed front destinations and perhaps side route numbers, but rear displays were generally abandoned. The advent of electronic displays changed all that and now, once again, buses are displaying front and rear service information, often with greater clarity than the linen blinds of old.

Despite operators' efforts to tell their passengers where each bus is going, some intending customers tend to look no further than the colour of the bus, as anyone who has driven a bus out of service past a waiting bus queue will testify. Indeed some intending passengers will attempt to flag down any bus – even when it is a different colour from the one they were expecting. This phenomenon is well illustrated by Lee Davis from his days at London Buses subsidiary, South London Transport. As Lee explains:

"In those days we operated a large number of day excursions and private hires using coach-seated Leyland Olympians and MCW Metrobuses. We also had three Routemasters fitted with tachographs and one of these was in a route 159 specific

Boarding passengers in the late 1970s, this OK Motor Services 78-seat Alexander-bodied Leyland PDR1/1 was new to Newcastle Corporation in 1961. OK didn't use route numbers and even went as far as painting "Bishop Auckland" on the upper destination glass. Otherwise immaculately turned out, the offside lower panels are in need of some attention.
(Geoffrey Morant)

Left: In all, 323 of these "small capacity" 35-seat ECW bodied Bristol SC4LKs were built between 1954 and 1961, of which Eastern Counties took 88. This 1957 example seen in Sudbury, unhelpfully showing 'service' instead of a destination name, was withdrawn within months of this 1971 view. It passed to contractors before conversion to a mobile home and export to Ireland in 1995. Behind it is a Thurgood-bodied Bedford SB1 belonging to Norfolk of Nayland. (Geoffrey Morant)

Below: Displaying a "Relief" destination, this 72-seat Park Royal-bodied AEC Regent V, below, is duplicating East Kent service 4 in Canterbury in 1975. Its all-over advertisement is promoting Rediffusion, a BET controlled company which originated as the Broadcast Relay Service in 1928 providing cable radio services. By the early 1970's Rediffusion was providing cable television and radio services to 1.3 million British households and had expanded to 14 overseas countries. (Geoffrey Morant)

livery of red and cream. One year we came up with the bright idea of running an additional trip to Brighton on what was normally a fortnightly shoppers service (number 612) to coincide with the Veteran Car Club London-Brighton run in November. To enter into the spirit of the occasion we decided to use one of the Routemasters.

"My driver and I proceeded to Brighton at a leisurely pace, many of the customers grateful for the chance to take photographs as we overtook the rally entrants. Our return pick-up was on Marine Parade, at the pier end of the Cliff Top. We duly pulled up a couple of minutes before time and loaded. An elderly lady then approached and given our Routemaster's colour scheme bore a passing resemblance to Brighton and Hove's distinctive red and cream livery, we should have guessed what might happen next. Seeing our bus displaying the number 612, but obviously not paying attention to the destination 'CROYDON' on the ultimate blind, she asked"

"Is this the same as the number 12? I want to go to Rottingdean."

"No, madam," I replied. "This is an express service to Croydon".

"Where?" she asked.

"Croydon", I repeated.

She looked at me blankly, "Where's that?"

"In South London," I informed her.

She gave me a horrified look, turned on her heel and, for a lady of advancing years carrying shopping bags in the rain, made a very fast exit in the direction of Rottingdean, looking over her shoulder in total disbelief several times as she went."

Below: Nowadays, there is much emphasis on emissions control but in the '50s and '60s big city smog (smoke + fog) could be a serious problem. Emerging from the murk in this 1964 Manchester scene is one of the Corporation's Metro-Cammell-bodied Leyland Atlanteans with an earlier Leyland, a Titan PD2 with Leyland bodywork, queuing behind. The use of the destination display FOG is explained on the previous page and is not an adjunct to the local weather reports. (Howard Piltz)

PTEGASAURUS

Sunday 26th October 1986 was a momentous day for buses outside London. The industry was commercialized, either by the creation of arms-length municipally, and PTA-owned, companies or by the imminent privatization of state-owned bus companies. The road service licensing regime was swept away. The Minister charged with implementing the legislation, Nicholas Ridley, was a Thatcherite who habitually confounded his political opponents with his blunt frankness.

Danny Marshall, Chairman of Tyne & Wear PTA, told me of one encounter where Danny and his colleagues had urged Ridley to hold a public consultation on the subject of their political disagreement. Ridley's reply was typically robust. "Why should I waste time doing that?" he retorted, "I won't agree with the results!" Geoff Inskip also told me of another Ministerial audience. This had been arranged by a Manchester Labour MP and convention dictated that Ridley could not refuse to meet them. He nevertheless made his stance perfectly clear throughout the meeting. While the delegation made its points, Ridley sat motionless with his head bowed, elbows on the table and hands covering his ears. Then when they had finished, he opened a folder on his desk and handed them a document. "Here's my reply," he said, "Thank you for coming to see me".

Love him or hate him, Ridley could not be faulted for making things happen. His fanciful vision was that every bus driver would have his own bus, in the style of some third world city but that was never going to happen, given the welter of "O" licensing, drivers' hours and vehicle safety regulation which remained in place. Nevertheless, the industry's management was for the first time set free to run its buses as it saw fit. No longer were they required to write reports so that other people could make decisions, they could now get on with it. Inevitably, the "big bang" caused market distortions. The new owners of privatized businesses had debt to pay back to the funders of their acquisitions. Early NBC disposals went for cheaper prices than later ones, as the Government consciously sought to kick-start

Post-deregulation competition in early 1990s Manchester was intense. Leading this Oldham Street procession is an A. Mayne and Sons 53-seat Seddon Pennine with Alexander bodywork new to Eastern Scottish in 1980, followed by a GM Buses Northern Counties-bodied Leyland Atlantean. Mayne was a long established independent operator which carried on regardless while competitive battles raged around it. The Bee Line Bus Company (BLBC) yellow double-deckers are 73-seat Park Royal-bodied Leyland AN68A/1Rs. Acquired in 1991, they were new to London Country in 1978. BLBC had been established by BET in 1986 to run minibuses in South Manchester but after acquisition by Drawlane, its focus shifted to double-deck operation on busier corridors. Once the Metrolink extension to Ashton was inevitable, Mayne sold its Manchester bus interests to Stagecoach in 2008. (Roy Marshall)

the disposal process. This put those at the front of the queue in a strong position to purchase subsequent disposals or to buy out newly privatized management teams who wanted to cash in their chips.

Some PTEs and municipals, in a bid to make their new bus companies more competitive, allowed any driving staff over 50 years of age to take voluntary redundancy and early pensions. In Manchester's case this wasn't even accompanied by more competitive rates of pay for any replacement new starters. The result was disastrous for GM Buses as hundreds of drivers came on to the labour market. With

pensions being paid and time on their hands, they made ideal recruits for a host of new start-up operations, offering much lower wages than the incumbent, which by then no longer had sufficient staff to run its registered services! Ridley couldn't have planned it better himself.

In many places, on-the-road competition was fierce, with, in some areas, an added frisson between drivers who had stayed to brave the new tomorrow, competing with their ex-colleagues who had taken their pensions and bought new cars with their pension lump sums. Some of the competitive tactics used bordered on criminality and don't bear repeating here, although anyone

Top: Competition in 1990s Liverpool was both colourful and plentiful. Liverbus of Huyton, established by four ex-Merseybus employees, initially ran a fleet of ex-GM Buses Leyland Atlanteans. Its first new buses were delivered in 1993 and 1994 and included this 76-seat Northern Counties Palatine II-bodied Volvo Olympian. In pursuit is a 74-seat Merseybus Leyland Titan, new to London Buses in 1982, with a Merseybus Leyland Atlantean on its tail. Also on view are Merseyline and Merseybus Atlanteans. After a period of intense competition, Merseybus acquired Liverbus in 1998 and, Arriva having purchased Merseybus in 2000, then acquired Merseyline in 2004. (Roy Marshall)

Left: London's £5 a day congestion charge was introduced in February 2003 and has since become £10. TfL reported three months later that traffic within the congestion chargeable, or "C" zone had reduced by 16% and public transport use had increased by 3%. Pictured in September 2012, this Abellio 69-seat Wright-bodied Volvo B7TL is entering the "C" zone at Upper Woburn Place. (Capital Transport)

In 2011 Oxford's main bus operators, Oxford Bus Company (OBC) and Stagecoach in Oxford introduced joint city service timetables, cutting buses by 25%, after environmental pressure from the County Council, and with the approval of OFT. This August 2012 scene in High Street shows the results with a Stagecoach 37-seat Alexander-bodied Dennis Dart SLF approaching. Also on view are two Alexander Enviro 400s, a blue Arriva 80-seat Dennis Trident and a red 70-seat OBC Scania N23, followed by a Thames Travel MCV 40-seat Evolution bodied MAN. Thames Travel was acquired by OBC in May 2011. (Malcolm Crowe)

who was around at the time will know of most of them. Local papers were full of "Bus Wars" stories and it was hardly the industry's finest hour. Yet within five years competition began to mature and looking back, what happened was an inevitable result of such seismic changes in the bus market outside London.

The 1990s brought consolidation and the emergence of the Groups and then, their stock exchange listings. This gave them access to new funding streams but also accountability to the stock market, which in turn gave them a new focus on how they were going to deliver organic growth in their businesses. By the start of the new millennium, marketing had moved up the industry agenda with the growing realization that filling empty bus seats had much in common with other modern retailing enterprises.

The deregulated bus industry had come of age and, by the 20th anniversary of deregulation in 2006, the product on offer was an infinitely better customer proposition than anything available in 1985. This was consistently confirmed by independent customer satisfaction research undertaken for the Department of Transport, and now under the stewardship of Passenger Focus. While there is no room for complacency and there remain pockets of poor performance, operators can now be justifiably proud of the quality of service they deliver, particularly when their passengers consistently score them more highly than London's contracted services on nearly every measure.

The recent Competition Commission Inquiry into the bus market outside London, which was a meticulous analysis of the industry's performance and behaviour, gave operators a largely clean bill of health. Why then, you might ask, are some Integrated Transport Authorities (ITAs) and their PTEs constantly lobbying via the publicly funded Passenger Transport Executive Group (PTEG) to implement London-style contracted regimes,

through the mechanism of Quality Contracts, first enabled by the Transport Act 2000?

It is not my intention to explore these issues here, but suffice it to say that these organizations are not working to the same agenda as their bus operators. The operators are seeking to grow their businesses by providing services their customers want with fast, reliable, frequent and affordable buses which can tempt motorists out of their cars for some of the journeys they are making. Fast journeys are about speedy fare collection and even more about priority on the highway, cutting the delays to buses caused by other traffic and parked vehicles. PTEs would agree but they are powerless to deliver on highway issues, where Metropolitan District Authorities are in charge and often have other agendas. This frustrates bus operators, particularly when they are forced to put more buses into schedules just to maintain reliability. "Doing nothing" on the urban highway degrades bus services and costs bus operators, and their passengers, both time and money.

Meanwhile, some of the ITAs and their PTEs continue to believe they should plan their bus networks and set fares, in some sort of pre-1986 Utopia. Then, they argue, services to customers would improve. They could ensure that all their council-tax payers had good access to buses, that fares would be the same throughout their areas, and they could somehow use the bus company profits to fund all this. They cite London as an example of what could be achieved, while conveniently forgetting that the London market is unique, with its high peak-hour commuter flows, its shortage of affordable parking spaces, its congestion charge, its increasing population, its reducing household car ownership and the hundreds of million pounds it spends on annual bus subsidies. Above all, they see their bus operators as a public utility providing a social service to their electors, not as market-focussed commercial enterprises which stand or fall by the relative attractiveness of their offering. It doesn't help that many of their elected members are committed motorists who use buses infrequently, if at all.

This continual friction, borne out of two differing ideologies, has held back the development of bus services in many ITA areas to the frustration of both parties. Bus operators point to the likes of Brighton, Cambridge, Nottingham, Oxford and York whose Authorities have been able to work in partnerships with their bus operators and have delivered integrated local bus, parking and traffic management solutions. These places have produced consistent and better bus services with impressive patronage growth at minimal cost to the public purse.

It was against this background that Brian Souter, Chief Executive of Stagecoach, was asked if he would speak at the Conference organized in Leeds to mark the 20th anniversary of deregulation. Noted for his forthright and entertaining speeches, Brian decided that he needed a memorable visual aid to support his presentation. The call went out to company Managing Directors, "Find me a dinosaur". The search began and it was not long before a resourceful MD was able to call Perth to advise that "the dinosaur is on its way", having located one which was surplus to requirements at Wookey Hole Caves.

On the day of the conference the dinosaur arrived early on the back of a Stagecoach stores wagon. It was decided that it should be taken for a stroll ahead of Brian's arrival and what better place to take it than a visit to PTEG's offices, which are in the West Yorkshire PTE building on Wellington Street, around the corner from the conference venue. The Director of PTEG, Jonathan Bray, is a seasoned campaigner who, in his day, has arranged many a publicity stunt. However, he was less than pleased to see his prehistoric visitor and greeted it and its minders with a string of profanities. Indeed, he was so upset that he called the police. An officer duly perambulated over to investigate the matter. On arrival, he looked the beast up and down and came out with the immortal words, "We don't get many of these round here." Having defused the tension, he asked the dinosaur's minders if they would move it on as it seemed to be distressing the gentleman from PTEG.

Point made, the dinosaur was taken to the conference venue and covered with a shroud so that Brian could unveil it during his presentation. And this is how he introduced it. "This creature is Ptegasaurus. It was discovered in 1968 having evolved from the dark mists of the 1960s lagoon. Since then it has almost single-handedly supervised, accelerated and acted as a catalyst for the decline in bus patronage in our major cities. Its habitat is large office buildings in metropolitan areas. It likes long chains of command and slow decision making. It feeds on large amounts of public funding and loss-making high profile projects. It is allergic to rapid change, modal shift, private sector ideas and serious bus priorities. For some inexplicable reason it is almost completely allergic to bus park and ride schemes". Brian continued, "What is the prognosis for the beast? It has never really adjusted to the deregulation asteroid which hit it in 1986 and it is probably facing extinction if it doesn't change. It is a dysfunctional quango which has failed dramatically to face the changing landscape we all now inhabit".

Brian went on to quote some metropolitan area statistics which demonstrated that the years for greatest passenger decline were in 1970 and 1971, when many smaller and efficient municipal operations were absorbed into the new PTE undertakings. His serious point was this. He wanted to see ideas and not ideology and he wanted to see genuine partnerships emerge which quickly addressed all of the issues which were preventing modal shift to buses in the metropolitan areas. It had already happened in a number of shire counties and it needed to happen in the conurbations too. I am sure that we would all drink to that.

A little bit of fun. This life-size prehistoric creature, dubbed "ptegasuarus," was used by Brian Souter to illustrate his speech at a "20 years of deregulation" conference in 2006. Seen here outside the Passenger Transport Executive Group (PTEG) Leeds offices, it is embracing a photograph of Gwyneth Dunwoody, MP for Crewe & Nantwich and long time chair of the House of Commons Transport Committee. Gwyneth, now sadly passed away, usually gave bus operator witnesses a hard time when they appeared before her Committee. (Stagecoach)

LONDON'S DIFFERENT

When the provinces were coming to terms with the brave new world of privatization and deregulation, London also began to adjust to a new but very different world, albeit at a different pace. Anyone who ever visited London Transport (LT) in the post-war years to learn how it did things would always find, before the conversation had gone very far, their hosts telling them, "Ah yes, but London is different."

To an extent that was true. Even after the transfer in 1970 of the Country Bus department (which operated in the Home Counties, more or less outside the area now bounded by the M25) and of Green Line to London Country Bus Services Ltd, a company formed by the National Bus Company for this purpose, London Transport still retained a fleet of some 7000 buses operated from around 70 garages. London was always good bus territory with its high population density, limited parking availability and high commuting peaks. But it also had the worst traffic congestion in the country and, when the economy was booming, enormous difficulty recruiting and retaining staff. However, some of its problems were self-inflicted, particularly given its tendency to adopt a "we know best" culture.

When the London Passenger Transport Board was created in 1933 its main bus operating constituent was the London General Omnibus Co. Ltd. London General had owned a subsidiary company, AEC, which provided virtually all its chassis requirements. AEC now had to become independent, but secured an agreement to supply ninety per cent of London's bus chassis. Body builder, Park Royal, was also to enjoy the lion's share of London's bus body requirements. From these stables came almost 10,000 of London Transport's two most famous buses, the RT and its successor, the RM and their derivatives. This standardization undoubtedly aided efficiency but was also at the root of later problems when London Transport switched to more conventional "bought in" buses in the 1960s and 70s.

Mark Yexley joined London Transport as a management trainee in 1979. He really wanted to make his career with London Underground, but colour blindness consigned him to the bus division, which was really struggling at the time. He recalls that some garages were losing as much as 35% of their mileage through staff shortages and engineering problems. While the rest of the UK had mastered the more demanding maintenance requirements of rear-engined double-deckers, London's two and a half thousand Daimler Fleetlines were proving to be a disaster. There were a number of reasons for this. LT had for many years relied heavily on its Chiswick chassis works and Aldenham body works to conduct major overhauls on each of its buses at four yearly intervals. In consequence, garage maintenance capabilities extended little further than running repairs. The "London knows best" culture had specified additional interlocks on doors and gears, which

Officially opened in 1956, Aldenham Works was originally intended to be an Underground Depot for a Northern Line extension which didn't happen. London Transport (LT) designed its buses so that body and chassis could be separated, with bodies overhauled here and chassis and running units overhauled at Chiswick, hence this 1980 line up of Routemasters, with engine and back axle sub-assemblies removed. RMC 2255 was built to Green Line specification and so passed to London Country in 1970, but had been re-purchased by LT in 1979. With modern buses unsuited to body/chassis separation and the abandonment of LT's four-yearly major overhauls in 1985, Aldenham closed a year later. (John Laker)

Facing page: The London General Omnibus Company made Chiswick its central maintenance works in 1921. The 32-acre site eventually included a half-mile test track and LT's driving school with this skid pan, which every trainee had to master. Around 7000 RTs and its derivatives were built, the last of which came out of service in 1979. This Park Royal-bodied example, RT 1530 saw service from 1949 to 1968 and after a period in store, became a Chiswick "skid bus" from 1980 to 1985. The Routemaster to the right was new in 1962 and after Green Line service, transfer to London Country and repurchase by LT, survived as a Chiswick training bus until 1990. (John Laker)

This page, top: London operated the largest trolleybus network in the UK with a peak of 68 routes and 1811 vehicles. The first trolleys entered service here at Fulwell in 1931 and the network finally closed in 1962 to be replaced by Routemaster buses. This AEC, 1385, pictured at the Stanley Road end of the depot, was one of a large 1939 order with chassisless construction by Metro-Cammell. Bomb damaged at West Ham works in 1944, a new East Lancs body was mounted on a new AEC 664T chassis. The Metrovick motors were replaced by English Electric but some of the AEC running units from the original were utilized in the new vehicle, which no doubt permitted it to be termed a rebuild. Entering service in 1948, it was withdrawn in 1960. (John Laker)

Centre: Designed jointly by LT and AEC, 2876 Routemasters (RMs) were built between 1954 and 1966. Their aluminium construction enabled a longevity that no one foresaw. This June 2003 Oxford Street scene includes three 64-seat RMs. The nearest, RM 1005, was new in 1962 and registered 5 CLT until 1991. It was withdrawn and sold in 1998 only to be repurchased two years later, re-engined and refurbished by Marshalls. The second is operating service 159, which was the last conventional RM-served route until 9th December 2005. Oxford Street has up to 600 buses an hour during the shopping day. (Capital Transport)

Left: London Transport's Mortlake Garage closed in 1983. To mark the 25th Anniversary of closure, this reconstruction was posed at Greater Manchester Transport Museum's London Bus Day in April 2008. The vehicle in the right foreground,(KGK 529) entered service in 1949 and is one of 500 all-Leyland RTWs – London's first 8ft wide buses. This particular example, RTW 29 is one of only 12 survivors. (Peter Nash)

everyone else managed without. These caused unreliability in operation. Demarcation between the various engineering trades meant that removing an engine from a vehicle took twice as long as anywhere else as mechanics waited for coppersmiths, who waited for electricians, who waited for bodybuilders, to each finish their tasks – and then they all stood around until they were required again. Finally, London's gruelling stop-start traffic conditions meant the Fleetlines went through gear boxes like they were going out of fashion. The Fleetlines weren't the first problem "foreign" buses bought by London Transport as over 1500 AEC Merlins and Swifts had been acquired between 1966 and 1972 and their withdrawal began as early as 1976.

Mark felt the problems ran deeper, however, as the whole organization was highly centralized and consequently rigid in its approach to the challenges it faced. He cited the Food Production Centre near Croydon, which was responsible for providing all the victuals needed in the seventy or so garage canteens right down to the last sausage, and the central Civil Engineering department which dealt with any premises issues. Works and Bricks, as it was called, didn't move particularly quickly and when it did eventually grind into action it was difficult to stop. Mark was at Edgware when the garage moved to new premises. Some considerable time before, Works and Bricks had been requisitioned to replace a bus-wash screen in the garage. A week before

the move they duly arrived and spent two days removing their hut from the lorry and generally setting up shop to undertake the work. They then took a lot of convincing, with phone calls back to HQ for instructions, before they could be finally persuaded that the job was no longer worth doing. He also recalls Works and Bricks arriving at Finchley to prepare for the installation of new cabling for an updated computer system. They arrived mob-handed but had only one masonry drill bit between them and this was of an enormous size that he had never seen before. By the time they had finished, the office walls resembled Swiss cheese with huge holes liberally sprinkled around the place.

London Transport has often struggled to recruit staff and in 1951 it decided to search for new recruits in Ireland. In 1956 it set its sights on Barbados and sought to encourage Caribbean hopefuls to come and work for it in the capital. With recruitment later extending to Trinidad and Jamaica, interviews were held in the West Indies and fares were paid for the passage to the UK. Some had difficulty acclimatizing to our alien world and Mark recalls talking to one long serving Barbadian conductor who vividly remembered the bitterly cold winter of 1963 with its heavy snowfalls, which he had never witnessed before. All driver training remained centralized at the driving school in Chiswick and the standards required far exceeded those necessary to drive modern automatic buses.

Mark reckoned that for every 100 applicants, ten would make it to interview, two would be accepted into the driving school and one-and-a-bit would eventually pass out as drivers.

When Mark arrived at Fulwell he was told tales of the trolleybuses when they ran from that garage. The vehicles themselves were mechanically simple and very reliable. Despite this there were teams of engineers employed to keep them on the road who invariably found that they had time on their hands so a routine was developed whereby they would often repair to the cinema when on late shift. They had the practice off to such a fine art that if they were required back at the garage in an emergency the projectionist would flash their team number up on the screen so that they could return to fix the problem, hopefully without missing too much of the film. LT had also installed an automated process for checking the trolleybus run-out which relied on a striker plate at the depot entrance picking up all trolleybus movements. This, in the days before CCTV, then enabled those in command at 55 Broadway to monitor what was happening in real time. One enterprising Inspector tried to beat the system by hitting the overhead striker plate with a conductor's bamboo pole but this caused the overhead to arc so severely that it welded the pole to the striker plate, stopping all bus movements until it could be removed.

The Greater London Council (GLC) was LT's controlling body when Mark started his LT career and Ken Livingstone, its leader, was soon to do battle with Margaret Thatcher and her incoming conservative administration. Mark recalls some strange things happening, like the unexpected arrival in the Stamford Hill garage union office of a large printing press which had been funded by the GLC, although they probably didn't realise it. He recalled that during the miners' strike the machine was working overtime printing leaflets and posters for the Socialist Workers' Party. In 1986 the GLC was abolished and London Regional Transport (LRT) was formed with the Government taking direct responsibility for the capital's transport system.

Some welcome changes were noted as LT embarked upon a process of preparing London Buses for privatization and anticipated deregulation. In 1985 services were, little by little, put out to tender and in 1988 the business was split into 11 separate operating companies as a precursor to removing centralized control. Each company began to develop its own personality and brand to go with it. Tendering meant that for the first time, platform staff and their trade unions were forced to face economic reality. Before this the centralized management structure had encouraged a centralized negotiating procedure with its London Bus Committee comprising management and trade union representatives drawn from depots and with full time officers. Mark recalls that even minor matters would get elevated through the negotiating structure, which would result in both delays to implementation and inevitable compromises. He recalls one attempt at renegotiating terms and conditions which management had introduced at the first meeting as "non negotiable". Many months later, when a compromise was eventually reached, one trade union official had remarked that they were the longest non-negotiable negotiations he had ever taken part in.

Tendering changed all this and, with the very real fear that work would be lost to incomers, staff productivity started to improve. As the tenders got bigger so did the risks that some of the new company managements were prepared to take. In 1991, the Managing Director of the 361-bus London Forest Company bid for work on the basis of a new set of drivers' terms and conditions. Having won the work he set about negotiating the new staff terms only to meet with stiff resistance from the employees. This led to a nineteen week strike, during which time LRT withdrew the awarded contracts and gave them to the second highest bidders, resulting in the eventual demise of the London Forest Company.

By 1994 the privatization process was underway and six of the ten remaining Companies were sold to existing operators outside London, while the other four were purchased by their management teams. This, together with the tendering process, achieved the desired effect, and in 1997/98 LRT was able to report that it had secured the whole network with minimal need for subsidy. And what became of deregulation? Mark believes that LRT's success in driving down the cost to the public purse of the London bus operation, the horror stories of bus wars in places like Manchester and the fact Government had its hands full in the 1990s with rail privatization, meant the appetite for it in Westminster was eventually lost.

But the absence of public funding wasn't to last, as wages were now too low and the quality of contracted services and the buses used to provide them left much to be desired, leading to a decline in patronage. In 1999, Londoners voted two to one in favour of an elected assembly and a Mayor to run its transport system. And so, in 2000, one Ken Livingstone became London's first Mayor (not to be confused with the Lord Mayor of the City of London, a ceremonial position which has existed since the days of Dick Whittington and his cat). The Mayor provides the policy direction for Transport for London (TfL) the body which took over operational responsibility from LRT.

Since then, the system of providing London's buses has developed. Ken Livingstone authorized a payment to all London bus drivers, known as the Mayor's bonus, to help operators overcome their staff shortages. The management buyout teams sold their businesses on to other operators as they found it increasingly hard to finance new vehicles which the new TfL contracts called for, nor did they have other UK operations to which they might cascade buses which could no longer meet the new tender criteria. The contracting regime became more sophisticated as Quality Incentives were introduced and then later refined. Today's London bus services are largely provided by a mix of British and European transport enterprises. Interestingly one operator, East Thames Buses was set up in 1999 by LRT itself to replace the services provided by a failed contractor, Harris Buses of Essex. Purportedly created to mop up any failed contracts and to ensure that contractors were not exploiting their

position it repeatedly came bottom of the league for performance and also made a loss, such that in 2009 TfL sold the business to London General, a Go Ahead Group subsidiary.

Having an elected Mayor at the helm of the capital's transport system keeps it in the political spotlight. The 2008 Mayoral election was in part fought over what type of high capacity bus should serve central London. Ken Livingstone favoured the articulated single-deckers which TfL had introduced to replace Routemasters on central area routes, while Boris Johnson promised a new bus for London (NBFL). This was to combine the latest hybrid technology with three entrances including the open rear platform of the much missed Routemasters. (The Routemasters had been finally withdrawn from mainline services in 2005). Having won the election, Johnson set about delivering his election commitment and in 2009 Wrightbus won the contract to build eight new hybrid vehicles, to enter service before the Olympic Games came to London in 2012. Once again, London argues that it has

This is LT2, the prototype new bus for London which entered service in February 2012. Following a design competition won by Thomas Heatherwick, the man who designed the 2012 Olympic flame, it was built by Wrightbus. It is powered by a Cummins ISBe 4.5-litre engine coupled to a Siemens hybrid transmission driving electric motors. The three entrance 66-seat configuration with an open (but closable) rear platform will accommodate 87 passengers. (Alan Millar)

led the way in developing new bus technology and in September 2012 TfL announced an order for a further 600 "Borismasters". These will be delivered between 2013 and 2016, but the contract price remains a closely guarded secret, suggesting that there will be few takers for new orders elsewhere. Indeed, earlier experience with the Routemaster, the last new bus for London, when only Northern General bought a batch of new vehicles, is most likely to be repeated. The "Borismasters" will also remain in the ownership of TfL, rather than its contractors, implying they are likely to stay in London for their entire service lives.

Finally, I asked Mark, given his experience of bus operations both inside and outside London, which he preferred. He told me that the service to passengers was infinitely better in London now than when he first joined London Transport, but it needed to be. The current London regime means that you only have one chance when you bid for a contract. If you get your calculations wrong, or your competitors have sharper pencils, then that is it – you lose the work at a stroke. In the provinces you have more options and you make your own luck. The success of your business is almost entirely down to you and your team's efforts and you are also responsible for every aspect of the product and its price.

So what of the endless debate about whether bus services outside London should all be contracted or not? It all boils down to the availability of public money and the political appetite to spend it on buses. DFT Transport Statistics 2011 and ONS Data show that London's current quality bus network costs £564m per annum, six times more per head of population than the average Metropolitan County area bus network. But everyone knows that London holds a special place in the nation's transport network. So will Metropolitan County electors be prepared to see a big rise in their Council Tax to pay for a franchised quality bus service regime where they live? You decide.

Transport for London (TfL), which sets the fares and decides the services in the capital, currently contracts services from three UK bus groups (First, Go Ahead and Stagecoach), three publicly owned European operators, German DB (Arriva), Dutch Railways (Abellio) and French RATP, as well as Singapore-based ComfortDelGro, French-based Veolia Transdev and a number of UK independent operators. The First Centre West 62-seat Wright Gemini-bodied Volvo B9TL was pictured at Charing Cross Station in August 2012. (Capital Transport)

THE VIEW FROM NORTH OF THE BORDER

From the mid 1970s the state-owned bus sector was committed to a comprehensive programme of network review. It was piloted at Midland Red in 1976 with the aid of NBC Consultancy Services and Colin Buchanan and Partners. The exercise was designed to establish which services could survive on their own two feet and which would need subsidy from the Local Authority if they were to continue. The study, which involved passenger attitude surveys, collecting data on every passenger trip, measuring bus speeds and monitoring reliability and then processing everything through central computers, was given the rather unglamorous title Viable Network Project (VNP). It took eighteen months to complete and was sufficiently successful for NBC to decide to roll it out across all of its subsidiaries under the slightly more subtle name of Market Analysis Project (MAP).

The MAP process was long overdue in many of the companies, which had failed to react comprehensively to rapidly reducing ridership. The system of analysis was undoubtedly sound, but was also lacking in that it ignored potential demand, instead concentrating solely on observed patronage.

It was then decided in Edinburgh that what had worked for NBC could work for the Scottish Bus Group, the sister to nationalized NBC in Scotland, and the exercise was rolled out there from 1979. Ian Manning tells this amusing story of his involvement with SCOTMAP as it came to be called. This is what he said:

"I was involved in the SCOTMAP Marketing Analysis Project from 1979 to 1981 and the first thing we had to do was to prepare all the journey survey sheets listing all the stops served on each journey which had had to be numbered with 5 digit codes and physically numbered on the stops for a temporary period so that the surveyors would recognize where they were. Weekend and evening work for me, despite being the number two in the department, was to go out in the SCOTMAP Ford Fiesta and stick the numbers on the stops. Given the rural nature of the Dundee, Angus and Kincardine

This 77-seat Alexander Northern, ECW-bodied Leyland Olympian LXB/1R photographed in Dundee was one of 21 which entered service in 1982. It passed to the new Strathtay Company in 1985, which was purchased by the Yorkshire Traction Group on privatization. Cab clutter can be an unsightly problem and this driver has elevated it to an art form. (Roy Marshall)

area, this involved trying to get the Fiesta off the road at bus stops on narrow lanes, before shinning up the poles with the self-adhesive numbers. This inevitably meant getting the car very dirty on verges and grassy banks.

"I took the car back to Dundee depot early one evening and asked the Depot Engineer, who had heavily accented speech, where the water tap or hose was. He replied that it was on the back wall so a very detailed scrutiny of the back wall located a hose in a holster and nothing else. It seemed quite elaborate for a water supply but as there were no other taps or pipes, I thought it had to be that. It was not until I had finished extensively spraying the car and noticing that there were a lot of bubbles in the water that I realized the liquid had a strong smell and a slight discoloration. I had sprayed the car with diesel! In a panic, I rushed to the Depot Engineer to tell him what I had done. He looked at me with his head on one side and said 'Aye well, son, it'll nae go rusty now!' When I asked him where the water actually was on the back wall, he pointed to a watering can in the corner . . . which only goes to prove how easily communications between Traffic and Engineering staff can go awry."

Today, Scotland's bus services are regulated in pretty much the same way as those in England and Wales, although there are minor differences in service registration regulations. Scotland also has its own Traffic Commissioner and a previous incumbent was Michael Betts. He was the man responsible for introducing the so-called 95% rule, against which Commissioners everywhere have since judged bus service punctuality. Mr Betts was presiding at a Public Inquiry when he asked one First Group manager what his target was for on-time operation. The Manager told him that it was 95%, which Betts immediately interpreted as an achievable national norm. Anyone who knows anything about running buses will tell you that, in urban situations, this is impossible and Traffic Commissioners up and down the land have since taken a lot of convincing that this is the case. Thanks Mr Betts.

Prior to deregulation, services were provided by the PTE in Strathclyde, municipal undertakings in Edinburgh, Dundee and Aberdeen, the Scottish Bus Group and

The Lothian Buses Air Link service runs twenty hours a day with a 10 minute frequency between 0630hrs and 0020hrs. This 80-seat Wright Eclipse Gemini 2-bodied Volvo B9TL is heading east on Edinburgh's Princes Street and, when pictured in April 2012, was running over the only section of tram track then evident in the city centre. (Alan Millar)

a large number of smaller independent operators. Today, only Edinburgh remains as a municipally owned company and apart from National Express in Dundee and over 200 independent operators, First Group and Stagecoach provide the majority of mainland and some island bus services.

Edinburgh's municipally owned operations, Lothian Buses, are both highly regarded and profitable. For how much longer this will be the case, is a matter for some conjecture. Edinburgh has embarked upon a tram project which has caused widespread consternation throughout Scotland's capital city and also raised some eyebrows south of the Border. Initially conceived in 2003 as a £375 million investment to link Newhaven with the Airport via the city centre, the scheme has been bedevilled with conflicts between contractors and the authorities and is running both late and out of money. By August 2011, it was admitted that the cost of building a little over half the system, the Airport to city centre section, would be a cool £776 million. Now the final bill is expected to exceed £1 billion when interest charges on the overspend are added. In September 2011 the decision was taken to abandon the Newhaven-Leith-City Centre section, which arguably presented the best

tram territory. The city's residents and traders on Leith Walk have suffered months of highway disruption while the statutory undertakers' pipes and cables were relocated in order to accommodate the tram tracks, which will not now materialize. The trams themselves have arrived and sit proudly in their new depot with nowhere to go, save one, which was for a while on public display in Princes Street.

Apart from the capital costs of creating the system, it was originally intended that any operating shortfall would be funded from Lothian Buses profits, though the commercial logic of this was never easy to grasp. While the frequent bus services on Leith Walk have been spared tram competition, the profitable AirLink 100 Express Service, now running every ten minutes for most of the day, will be hit hard if, and when, the trams start running. That can

All locked up with nowhere to go – apart from a short test track here at Gogar Depot, 24 of Edinburgh's 27 Spanish CAF-built trams were delivered in 2010 and 2011. Contractual disputes and cost overruns have resulted in a truncated network and a lengthy delay to opening with passenger service not expected to start before 2014. (Peter Nash)

In 1995 Series 2 Leyland Nationals operated the majority of services on Arran, provided by Stagecoach Western under contract to Strathclyde Passenger Transport. Having just met the ferry from Ardrossan, this 1980 52-seat example is departing Brodick with a good load of visitors for Brodick castle. (Geoffrey Morant)

only mean that Lothian Buses profits will fall, thereby reducing the Company's ability to fund the tram operating deficit!

Of course, it was all meant to be so different. Edinburgh initially planned to introduce a congestion charging scheme with the proposition that the money raised from motorists would be used to fund public transport improvements and particularly the tram scheme. Eventually the proposal was put to residents in a referendum in 2005 and resulted in a resounding 75% "no" vote. The "yes" campaigners weren't helped when, in the run up to the referendum, the council declared that the tram scheme would go ahead anyway – whatever the referendum vote! One wonders whether the city McFathers had known then what we all know now, they would have been quite so enthusiastic in their endorsement of what is popularly regarded to be Scotland's biggest white elephant.

Folks in the Highlands and Islands regard themselves as a little more streetwise than their cousins in Edinburgh. Visitors are carefully monitored, none more so than visiting officials whose arrival would be signalled in advance by vigilant ferry crews. It was often said that one bus operator on Skye used to run his buses on slave tyres but when the man from the Ministry arrived to inspect them another set of wheels with new tyres would be

miraculously installed for the duration of the visit and associated inspection.

Robert Andrew is a Scot who was brought up in the Highlands, where everyone knows everyone else and their business. He should therefore have no excuse for one unguarded experience on Arran, which led him to make the front page of the local paper. His story goes like this.

"In autumn 1992 I was working my notice for Western Buses prior to joining Stagecoach. The company had successfully won tenders on the island of Arran to operate the local services and school services previously operated by Arran Transport. I spent two weeks on Arran, one either side of the launch, training the newly recruited Controller and his staff in our processes and enjoying some spells driving. Leyland National Mark 2s were the mainstay of the fleet, supplemented by three Dodge minibuses for schools work.

"The tenders were operated under contract to Strathclyde Passenger Transport (SPT), who had a presence on the island at "go live" to ensure that we were meeting our commitments. The fleet of nine Nationals and three Dodges was somewhat challenging and on the Sunday evening prior to the first Monday's operation, one National was "dead" with serious defects, one would not start, and one would not stop. With a spare allocation of 2 buses, we ended up with a bus running at an outstation all night since any maintenance back up was a ferry journey away and they had stopped running for the night!

"Somehow we got through the launch OK, but I then inadvertently and innocently managed to make front page news on the local newspaper, the Arran Banner. One of the SPT officials was a former colleague from Kelvin Scottish, so we arranged to meet for a meal and a pint in a local hotel to have a friendly catch up. Our presence was observed by some locals, no doubt with sympathies for Arran Transport, who immediately put two and two together to come up with five. The newspaper loved it and

headlined a conspiracy theory about stitched up tender awards. Time moved on, and Stagecoach subsequently bought Western in 1993. It continues to operate the contracts to this day, with a somewhat more reliable fleet than I inherited in 1992."

Gordon Hanning, recalling his time as Transport Co-ordinating Officer in Fife, told me of an incident where he became involved with one of the first Stagecoach vehicles to be fitted with CCTV cameras there. The bus concerned had been comprehensively trashed on a school run and now, for the first time, it was possible to identify the perpetrator. Gordon and the school became involved and the culprit was identified on tape in glorious high-definition colour. The head teacher contacted the boy's parents and the father, who had "Hey Jimmy" tendencies, became increasingly aggressive and denied vehemently that his son would ever do such a thing. A meeting was arranged at the school with both father and son present and father once again protested his son's innocence. He was then shown the CCTV footage and with one bound was across the room and began knocking six bells out of his beloved child. Gordon says it took all the adults in the room to restrain him and prevent the lad receiving a serious hiding.

News travelled fast and needless to say, there were no more vandalized buses at that particular school although Gordon reckoned

Rennies Lion Coaches began providing contract services for miners and for HM Dockyard, Rosyth, from its Cairneyhill base in 1948. Following a merger with Comfort Coaches in 1963, its name was changed to Rennies of Dunfermline. Expanding rapidly after deregulation, it was acquired by Stagecoach in 2007. Rennies also traded extensively in second-hand buses and this is one of fifty-five 76-seat Alexander bodied Leyland Atlantean AN68/1Rs built in 1973 and purchased from Greater Glasgow PTE in 1988. Rennies have added the strengthening bar supporting the upper front windscreen. (Geoffrey Morant)

that some Scottish school kids would be worthy contestants in the Vandalism Olympics. He recalls how Rennies of Dunfermline were forced to fit external strengthening bars to the upper front windscreens of thirty double-deckers after the kids had worked out how to push the windows out. He also remembers other video nasties where the children were all rushing to one side of the top deck as the bus negotiated a corner, in the (unsuccessful) hope that they might tip it over, and one not so wee bairn who brandished a homemade flame thrower.

Meanwhile, Robert Andrew remembers one embarrassing incident where he managed to "lock out" his new boss, Brian Souter. It happened like this.

"Not long after I joined Stagecoach in November 1992, the Rapson service between Inverness and Forres was purchased. This allowed us to create the new Bluebird Service 10 linking Aberdeen and Inverness via Elgin, a distance of 105 miles, which for Northern Scotland is not exceptional. In early May 1993, along with Alisdair Goodall, I was in the cash office at Inverness Depot programming the Waycon ticketing system with the new fares in readiness for service 10's launch. We heard a faint knock on the door. It was a Thursday, the normal visiting day for the commercial advertising company we used in that area

and their representative, who could talk for Scotland, would have delayed our progress on the fares work considerably. We therefore decided to ignore the knock, and did so twice more. Finally the phone rang, which Alisdair answered, so I succumbed and opened the locked cash office door, to find Brian Souter standing on the other side. This was the first time I had met Brian who was making an unannounced visit to see how his new local Manager was getting on.

"That incident apart, I thought the visit went well. We then spent some time viewing buses from the window of McDonalds, where we could observe the key local services. It later transpired that the phone call when I opened the door was from Liz, now my wife, desperately trying to alert us that it was Brian who was seeking an audience with me."

Post-deregulation competition in Inverness hit the national headlines in 1990, when state-owned Highland Scottish Omnibuses (HSO) was found guilty of anti-competitive behaviour by the competition authorities. Rapsons, a local coach operator, with others, acquired the HSO business in 1991 and by 1998 it had succeeded, through a series of acquisitions, mergers and demergers in building a network which covered the Highlands, Orkney and Skye. In May 2008 it sold the business to Stagecoach. This 2002 70-seat Plaxton-bodied Dennis Javelin, was just weeks old when recorded at Inverness after completing its journey from Aviemore. (Geoffrey Morant)

THE WARM HEART OF AFRICA — A TRILOGY

PART 1 — INTO AFRICA

In March 1989 Stagecoach made its first overseas acquisition when it purchased a 51% stake in United Transport Malawi Limited from United Transport International, a BET subsidiary. Brian Cox recalls his experiences immediately post acquisition…

"Stagecoach's purchase of United Transport Malawi took the bus world completely unawares. It was cheeky enough that the Scottish upstarts had bought into the NBC two years earlier … but Africa? Brian Souter sent me over soon after the acquisition saying, "take your wife Anne with you, show we're a caring, family business … but, eh, make sure you travel economy, won't you?"

"So we landed in Malawi – our first time in Africa – and after some induction at UTM's Head Office in Blantyre, set off for a Grand Tour of the "Warm Heart of Africa" with its friendly people and superb landscapes. Patrick, a local senior manager, acted as our guide and driver. No one from Stagecoach had yet been north of Lilongwe, Malawi's new capital, so we felt like (somewhat apprehensive) pioneers, albeit cocooned in the luxury of the company's 4WD Pajero.

"Patrick's driving seemed OK, thankfully, given African roads and the hordes of people using them as footpaths, and it was only later that we learned he had (allegedly) something of a track record, probably not unconnected with his – clearly well-connected – father having (again allegedly) arranged a driving licence for him without the inconvenience of having to sit a driving test. Anyway, this story isn't about Patrick's driving, as you'll see.

"We duly proceeded north, making a first stop in Kasungu to look at the local facilities. By this time, fresh to Africa, Anne also pretty desperately needed facilities, to everyone's consternation. After a huddle, she was led off to the staff toilets, which were supposedly rather better than the bus station loo, the local supervisors probably nevertheless fearing for their futures. After what seemed rather a long time, she eventually re-emerged, broke into a big grin and brandished an unused sample

Malawi has a population of 14.9 million, 90% of whom live in rural areas. Ranked 12th poorest country in the world, its land area is about 90% that of England. It borders Lake Malawi, the world's eighth largest lake, for 360 miles. With only 9600 miles of roads, less than half of them metalled, progress can be both slow and treacherous in the November to May rainy season. Every vehicle needs all terrain capability and buses, which were either ERF Trailblazers or Leyland Victories, were sufficiently ruggedized to be able to continue their journeys if hauled out of a ditch. (Brian Cox)

of local loo paper – a strip off a Setright roll! She probably still has it somewhere. Decorum requires the rest be left to the reader's imagination. (As I recall, I managed to survive until we got to a hotel that evening. Lesson Number One: always take …).

"We reached Mzuzu in the north and then dropped down to Lake Malawi to head back south along its shore. Those who have been to Malawi will know how beautiful the whole country is, but the Lake is particularly lovely and we were looking forward to the trip (this is work? I thought). Until now the roads, if not always wonderful (in fact, a bit like potholed Britain circa 2012), had at least been tarred, but at that time the Lakeside road was still dirt, or in parts mud in this case, as the rainy season had barely come to an end.

"We worked our way down the Rift Valley Escarpment to the Lake, and proceeded gingerly southward, admiring the scenery. At some point – I can't remember exactly where – the road surface became atrocious. Patrick explained that the main rains had ended and the road had largely dried out, but it had then rained again causing the top layer to turn back to mud, making it a bit like an icy road starting to melt and just as difficult to cope with.

"Not long after, we came round a bend to see one of our buses in a ditch, clearly having slid off the road. Around it stood its load of passengers, including some white South African girl tourists (some of whom turned out to be suffering from malaria and were not at all

well), its driver … and a driving instructor, who looked very, very sheepish indeed.

"Well, you've probably guessed what had happened: the driver had been struggling with the slippery surface, so the instructor (and I can't now remember, if I ever knew, why he was there that day) had said, 'look, you'd better let me take over', or maybe even 'let me show you how to do it'. According to the passengers, he was barely behind the wheel before he put the bus into the ditch and now one of his own senior managers had turned up out of the blue, with two representatives of the new owners to boot. No wonder he was sheepish.

'What happens now, then?' I asked. 'We'll have to wait until we can get the breakdown truck up', I was told, either from Nkhotakota several hours down the Lake, or even right back from Lilongwe. Either way, it was going to be a long, long wait, especially for impatient Europeans and South African girls with malaria. 'Isn't there anyone nearer able to pull us out?' I asked. 'Well, there's the Lonrho plantation down the road,' I was told. 'They've got a digger.' I turned to Patrick and said, 'Right, let's go down there and see if they'll help.' 'We can't do that,' someone said. 'The manager will have to approve it, and he'll be the middle of his long siesta – no-one is allowed to disturb him.' That was enough for me. 'Get that car started, Patrick', I said.

"And, of course, the Lonrho manager was delighted to see us, despite being woken up, and couldn't have been more helpful. In no time the bus was out of the ditch and both we and the bus were on our ways. (Lesson Number Two: well, there was a lesson there somewhere, but as this was Africa, I'm not entirely sure what it was!).

"Later that day, nearer Lilongwe (his home), Patrick bought a basket of freshly-caught fish from a local fisherman and placed them on the back seat alongside Anne in a stifling temperature; it's a wonder she ever recovered! Ah Africa!"

THE WARM HEART OF AFRICA

PART 2 – IN AFRICA

In 1991 BET decided to divest all of its remaining worldwide local bus operations and Stagecoach acquired a 75% share of Kenya Bus

Services (Nairobi) and a 51% share of Kenya Bus Services (Mombasa), thus giving the Group responsibility for bus operation in another African nation.

Apart from the difficulties encountered negotiating highways, graphically described by Brian Cox above, there were a number of practical problems to address which never arise in the UK. For instance, it was found that engineering staff were physically unable to undertake the sort of manual handling work common in British workshops, principally because they were seriously undernourished – a problem which was addressed through the provision of proper canteen meals and balanced diets. It was also not unknown for drivers to abandon their vehicles and disappear into the bush with their takings, having not seen such large (to them) sums of money before. In some areas AIDS was endemic and the Company extended training into the broader area of Health Education with demonstrations of how to use a condom with aid of a banana.

Staff enthusiasm was high but it was patently clear that additional training for both drivers and managers was necessary, and instructors were seconded from the UK to set up programmes in order to train the African trainers. As Bill Davies explains, even staff training held some unexpected pitfalls...

"In 1996 I was involved in arranging and delivering the third management training programme to our colleagues in Stagecoach Kenya and Malawi. To the delight of the team

of presenters the first two days went extremely well with active and often very vociferous participation from the group. On the third day, I was timetabled to lead the first session of the morning dealing with company structure and the role of management.

The first 30 minutes or so passed well, again with a high level of group participation. As I was writing up key points on the flip chart, I started to introduce the next part of the session. A few seconds had passed before I realized that, for the first time since the conference had started, a total silence had descended. Turning from the flip chart I found to my dismay that I was looking at 37 totally uncomprehending faces! What had I said? Why was everyone looking perplexed? A few more seconds – or possibly an eternity – passed before the penny dropped. I had just said that, to their customers, companies were like icebergs in that the greater part of the structure was hidden from view.

"Apparently icebergs do not offer instant, nor indeed any, mental imagery if you live in sub-Saharan Africa. It's obvious, of course, but it wasn't to me at the time. It might have been a

This is Lilongwe's busy bus station. Services ran from here to every part of the country. Passengers could bring any luggage they wished, including livestock and furniture, so long as they could get it onto the roof rack and secure it safely. Often they would choose to ride on the roof to protect their possessions. The tariff for carrying goods was based on size, not on weight or value. (Nigel Barrett)

good analogy, but in this locale it was definitely the wrong sort of weather! Fortunately a request to the kitchen for a glass of water and an ice cube rescued the situation but that brief amusing and embarrassing moment when I 'died' in front of an audience is a Stagecoach memory that I will never forget."

The cultural differences were also brought home to the staff in South Shields when a rising-star management trainee came over to Scotland for the 1995 Annual Stagecoach conference. Before returning to Africa he spent a week on Tyneside observing how a British Stagecoach depot operated. Reporting on the visiting trainee's performance, Dave Shaw, the Divisional Manager stated he was impressed by the knowledge of his young charge. They had even taken him shopping so that he could return home with a UK souvenir as a present from the staff.

The youngster had surprised them all, when he had asked the price of chickens. Trying to help, they had enquired whether he meant frozen chickens, fresh chickens or ready-cooked chickens, to be told, "No – live chickens". On further questioning it transpired that in his homeland chickens were common currency and he was frantically trying to price the trainers, which he really wanted to be his gift, in a currency he could understand!

THE WARM HEART OF AFRICA

PART 3 – AND OUT AGAIN

By 1997 the Stagecoach adventure in Africa was coming to a close. The highways infrastructure was failing and consequently operating conditions were becoming more and more difficult. The company also had to cope with illegal competition. The bus service regulatory regime in Kenya and Malawi was not unlike that operating in the UK before 1980 and, as the major operator, the Company was required to adhere to the rules. However, there were rapidly growing fleets of illegal minibuses

ranged against it, which the Authorities studiously ignored. Faced with a population unable to pay realistic bus fares, illegal minibuses stealing those passengers who could, and inadequate highways, the Group decided to call it a day. Nigel Barrett was in charge in Malawi at the time and recalls disposing of the Malawi operation to the Government for the princely sum of 1 Kwacha, (about 2.4p).

Nigel also well remembers the support the Company had received from the Malawi government and in particular one wage negotiation which had been conducted from the back of a pick-up truck in the middle of Blantyre Depot. The claim was for a mere 2000% increase in pay and the majority of the depot's drivers encircled the pick-up. However, this was not as intimidating as might first appear, since ringing the depot was a contingent from the Malawian army, each member of which was armed. While Nigel doesn't recall the deal reached, it was settled there and then to the company's satisfaction, and without any loss of life.

Shortly before the disposal of the Company, Nigel decided to send the driver-trainers seconded from Inverness back to the UK. Their African driver-training counterparts resolved that they should not leave without a farewell party and duly took them off into the bush for a final night out. They partied well into the night and when the time came to leave, one young African lady wanted to come with them. The Malawian hosts strongly advised against such an outcome – advice which was heeded. However, on the return journey it transpired that the advice had been given not on health or moral grounds, but because the young lady had wanted to charge 20 Kwachas for her company, which the hosts regarded to be more than excessive.

Brian, Nigel and Bill all agree that Malawi had been much-loved by those who had been involved and that Stagecoach had made bus services there amongst the best in Africa. As Brian concludes, "This episode was just one of the many things that made Stagecoach such a delightful company to work for, especially in the early days before we had the City looking over our shoulders at every move we made".

BUGGY WARS

I don't suppose that when the Department for Transport (DFT) or whatever it was then called, started its drive to make the nation's bus fleet low-floor, that it envisaged the difficulties operators might face in dealing with young mums battling for their share of any available buggy space. The low-floor requirement, which must be met by all single-deck buses in 2015 and double-deckers in 2017, will be challenging for the industry. Yes, we know that we have had years to prepare for it but nobody foresaw that the money would run out. The problems will be felt most keenly by shire county Local Authorities, where secured service budgets are already at full stretch. There are many secured rural services which are still provided by Mercedes step-entrance minibuses with a passenger capacity exceeding 22, where the upgrade to low-floor replacements will be the straw that breaks the camel's back. For the luckless passengers on these services it is likely to be a case of no service at all. I am sure that if they were asked whether they preferred a step-entrance bus or no bus, these passengers would opt for the former but the law is the law.

The majority of today's urban services are already operated by low-floor buses, which have room for both buggies and wheelchairs. The problem for bus operators is that the former tend to outnumber the latter by around 100 to 1. In some areas young mums rule OK, and their buggies are invariably the perambulating equivalent of a Range Rover. Three of these aboard and drivers have a real problem on their hands if a wheelchair passenger, or a fourth large buggy seeks to join the party. There are of course, statutory notices on display advising buggy pushers to cede the space to wheelchair users but the evidence is that many mums in inner city areas can be decidedly territorial, even when drivers have politely asked them to fold up their baby carriages. I have even heard one report from Liverpool of violence breaking out between competing mothers and the police having to be called.

These problems, or at least the problem of space on buses for push chairs, are nothing new. Robin Orbell tells of his days as Assistant Traffic Superintendent in Bath in the early 1970s. The city was the destination for a number of country bus services which in those days were operated by elderly ECW-bodied

This immaculate 1964 45-seat ECW-bodied Bristol MW5G is seen operating Bath Services in 1969. Heading in the opposite direction is a Plaxton-bodied Black and White coach on Associated Motorways duties. (Geoffrey Morant)

Bristol LS6Gs. They were fine vehicles but had next to no luggage space over the front wheel arch. The Company's plan to overcome this was ingenious. The message went out to mums, bring your child, but leave your pushchair at home. Buy a return ticket and when you get to Bath come and exchange it for one of our push chairs. When you are ready to go home, bring back the pushchair and we will swap it for your return ticket.

The scheme worked so well that Robin was despatched as a fresh-faced young man to buy extra pushchairs. He found a shop which specialized in such wares and was ushered in by the blue-rinse lady who ran the place. He explained that he was looking for pushchairs and she proceeded to show him her available range starting, as all good sales people do, with the most expensive. Having had a full explanation of all the features of the particular vehicle, Robin said it wasn't quite within his price range and asked if she had anything cheaper. The process repeated itself until they eventually reached the entry model. By this stage, the shop owner was a little downhearted but still excited to be making a sale to what she believed was a slightly embarrassed, expectant young father. Robin says he remembers the lady's reaction to this day, when he said, "I'll take this one. Can I have three of them please?"

With increasing enquiries about the carriage of mobility scooters, in 2006 Stagecoach carried out field trials in Chesterfield with the help of a local retailer, on a number of different types of buses and scooters to establish which it could safely carry. This electric wheelchair had no difficulty manoeuvring on an Optare Solo or a Dennis Dart. (Peter Nash)

Blue Bus of Horwich, formed by two ex-Shearing managers, started a service between Horwich and Bolton in 1991. It expanded significantly in the Bolton and Wigan area and started to run a service into Manchester until acquired by Arriva in 2005. This 27-seat Plaxton Beaver-bodied Mercedes 0814 was new in 2002 and is bedecked here in a celebratory livery to mark the Queen's Golden Jubilee. Its non-DDA compliance means that use on local bus services will become unlawful on 1st January 2015. (Roy Marshall)

ROYAL VISITS

Royal visits come in two sizes – official and unofficial. Official visits in the transport world tend to be associated with grand openings of new systems and invariably involve months of planning meetings, dry runs and carefully timed itineraries. It is well known that when Her Majesty the Queen, accompanied by the Duke of Edinburgh, is cutting the tape or unveiling a plaque, that His Royal Highness takes great delight when something happens which wasn't in the script. Bob Hind recalls just one such occasion in Cheshire.

In the early seventies Runcorn New Town and its revolutionary Busway attracted visitors from around the world who wanted to see if this Liverpool overspill development with its pioneering bus network really did work. At its centre, Shopping City was still pristine and sparkling when the Queen was invited to officially open the new development. The great and the good were to be gathered to meet Her Majesty and the Duke of Edinburgh and planning meetings addressing the visit filled the diary for months in advance of their arrival. It was decided that the Royal party should drive along the Busway to see some of the housing communities and arrive in Shopping City at one of the bus platforms from where they would descend by escalator to the shopping area to perform the formalities.

Whilst it was never a concern that Her Majesty would show any interest in the bus network, Crosville, the operating company, and the officials of the Development Corporation wanted to make sure that the Queen would realize that her point of arrival was, in fact, the central bus station. It was therefore decided to 'discreetly' place a bus at the far end of the platform, well away from where the Royal Party would disembark and where it would cause the least interest. No one had considered Prince Phillip's notoriety and downright devilment for deviation from the Royal itinerary.

The great day arrived and officials gathered on the bus platform to welcome the Royal Party. The Queen and her Escort duly arrived and were carefully ushered towards the escalator. At the last moment Prince Phillip noticed the bus and made a bee-line for it. A look of panic simultaneously spread over every face and Peter Jenner, one of Crosville's Head Office contingent, raced ahead of the Duke and

When Arriva acquired British Bus, it became the successor to Crosville in Cheshire and incumbent operator on the Runcorn Busway. The vehicle seen here is a 1995 40-seat East Lancs 2000 bodied-Dennis Dart. East Lancashire Coachbuilders of Blackburn went into liquidation in 2007, later to become part of the Optare Group in 2008. In 2012 production in Blackburn ceased and all work was transferred to the newly-built Sherburn in Elmet production facility near Leeds.
(Ken Swallow)

jumped into the driver's cab of the bus – no doubt because he feared that the Duke might attempt to drive the vehicle away. The Duke climbed on to the platform of the bus to be greeted by a smiling Peter. The Duke glanced down into the driver's cab which was strewn with cigarette butts. He looked Peter in the eye and said "Don't you provide your drivers with ashtrays?" Before waiting for a reply from the dumbstruck Peter, he turned, with a glint in his eye, to return to the waiting Monarch.

Unofficial visits have a totally different complexion and usually arise when some disaster has taken place and a member of the Royal family drops in to commiserate with those who have had to cope with an unexpected crisis. In circumstances such as these no preparations are necessary and the visiting dignitary gets to see life as it really is. Nigel Barrett hosted one such visit in 2005 at the Stagecoach depot in Carlisle.

Shortly after 5am on Saturday 8th January 2005, Nigel was awoken by a phone call to alert him that the early-turn supervisor was unable to reach Willenhall Depot as the access road was impassable under four feet of water. Heavy rainfall and a spring tide had together caused the nearby river to back up and burst its banks and the whole area was already submerged including the Depot. The waters continued to

rise as the management team met at the bus station. Radio Carlisle was asked to broadcast that bus services were suspended and to ask bus drivers to report to the bus station. Much of the town centre was flooded and the only "traffic" was the Coastguard inflatables which were busily rescuing marooned residents from their houses. By 11.30 all power was lost and mobile phone reception became erratic as the radio announced that the floods would peak at 3pm. Six buses were brought from Penrith via the A6, the only passable route into the town and these began operating to Harraby and Upperby, the only unaffected areas. Even these routes were becoming impassable and as a full scale evacuation was now underway four buses were diverted to provide transport to the reception centres which were being set up.

A call had already gone out to other Stagecoach companies for vehicles and on the Sunday 45 buses were dispatched from Scotland, the North East and Manchester together with ten from the West Cumbria reserve. The owners of Kingmoor Park on the outskirts of Carlisle had kindly offered parking space for the relief fleet and this was to become the new operating centre for the next four weeks with a temporary portakabin installed that day.

Monday's run-out was controlled chaos, but an emergency timetable was operated on all services. Driving instructors stood by to familiarize drivers with the controls on "foreign" vehicles and hand-made destination displays were installed at the bus station. A 35,000 litre temporary fuel tank was also arranged, but until its arrival on Wednesday, an account was set up with a BP filling station, to which all drivers took their vehicles en-route to Kingmoor via the M6 Motorway. Meanwhile access had eventually been gained to the depot, which was a scene of utter devastation. The waters had reached a depth of six feet and buses had been lifted and then dumped around the site. An articulated lorry and caravans had also been washed onto the premises. The pits were full of water and the whole place was a mixture of water, silt, oil and sewage from the sewage works half a mile away.

By Tuesday a full registered service was operated and the electronic equipment needed to programme the destination blinds had been brought in together with a portable wash from North East. News for the depot was that it would be some time before it would become habitable again, so a further call for vehicles was made yielding a further 18 buses from further afield, allowing some of the initial intake to be returned. Depot staff were working eighteen hours a day on the depot clean up and a total of 85 vehicles was written off by the insurers who assembled a fleet of recovery vehicles to remove them to North Staffordshire. Amongst them were seven stored London Routemasters, which mysteriously found their way back into circulation once the insurers had taken responsibility for them.

And amongst all the chaos at the Depot in walked Prince Charles, who had come to Carlisle to see the devastation and to meet those who had suffered. After talking to displaced residents and those who had rescued them, he came to Willenhall to thank the staff for their sterling efforts in getting the show back on the road so quickly. There was certainly no looking for cigarette butts in drivers' cabs on this occasion.

January 2005 and Prince Charles arrives at the Stagecoach Willenhall depot unannounced to hear at first-hand how staff got the show back on the road after Carlisle's floods. While he hears just exactly how it was, a colleague wonders whether 'too much information' is wise! All must have been well, however, for the Prince was impressed and thanked all concerned for their efforts. (Nigel Barrett)

THE BARE-CHEEKED MAYOR & THE CLOCK THAT STOPPED AT MIDNIGHT

Stagecoach has always been willing to explore new business opportunities, no matter where they have arisen. It invariably fell to Brian Cox to undertake the initial research and this tale recounts his involvement in an exciting prospect to develop a new busway system in Bogotá, the capital of Colombia, South America. As Brian explains:

"Still active today, but sadly recently diagnosed with Parkinson's Disease, Antanas Mockus was one of the colourful politicians that Latin America seems to throw up with surprising frequency – think Argentina's Menem, Peru's Fujimori, and more recently Venezuela's Chávez, not to speak of Abdalá Bucaram of Ecuador (who actually campaigned as "El Loco", the madman) and his dancing girls. Few of them seem to have bestowed worthwhile legacies on their countries but Colombia's Mockus is an exception. Along with his successor as Mayor of Bogotá Enrique Peñalosa, he must take much of the credit for the developments that have transformed Bogotá in recent years. Most important of these must surely be the modern Transmilénio bus network introduced in 2000 under Peñalosa - who had recommended such a scheme as far back as 1985. This has made a huge contribution to reducing the City's previous traffic chaos, and

which Mockus further developed when he returned for a second term.

"One day in 1994 I got a call – another of those calls – from Brian Souter, saying, 'I need you to go to Colombia tomorrow – can you make it?' Dumbfounded, I could only reply, 'well, yes, of course'. 'Actually, you'll need to go to Brazil first,' he went on, 'and meet some guys from Volvo, and then go on to Colombia. Eh … and you can go Business this time'. Must be important then, I thought. And so began 18 months of shuttling back and forth to Colombia and Brazil. In the end, nothing came of it for Stagecoach, which was with hindsight perhaps for the best at that time, as some of the possible scenarios hardly bear thinking about, but we all learned a lot.

"Back then, we in Britain knew little about a city in Brazil called Curitiba or its modern bus system pioneered by visionary mayor Jaime Lerner, but the rest of Latin America was already familiar with it, not least Bogotá. With a population of five million by the early 1990s and still growing rapidly (it's nearly double that now), with no metro, a chaotic bus system,

Steam train excursions are as popular in Bogotá, Colombia as they are in the UK. However on this occasion the American-built Baldwin steam engine came to grief before the party reached their destination. (Brian Cox)

Segregated, simple and successful: Curitiba Express buses began operating on a 37-mile network of segregated corridors in 1992. The 24.5 metre Volvo bi-articulated buses, which seat 57 and have crush loads of 270, operate at three minute peak headways. (Alan Cannell)

Facing page: Before its busway network was built, central Bogotá was wall-to-wall buses; this 1994 scene is reminiscent of London's Oxford Street today. (Brian Cox)

and located in the Andes at over 8,500 feet, Bogotá suffered from appalling congestion and pollution. Poor government, shortage of funds and difficult geological conditions had defeated several efforts to build a metro, and the situation was becomingly increasingly acute.

"Another Jaime, Jaime Castro, who was the City's Mayor from 1992 to 1994, realizing that a Metro remained unfeasible but that it had still many supporters, decided to run an open competition. This would not only to give metro proponents their say, but also to try to overcome the vested interests of the large number of existing bus operators, who were doing very well thank you with the status quo. This is where Volvo and Stagecoach came in. Volvo already had a factory in Curitiba and supplied buses there, including bi-articulated vehicles, the latest development. Bogotá represented a great opportunity but Volvo Bus needed a credible operating partner and looked to one of their biggest customers, Stagecoach. As the tender required local involvement Volvo

had already hitched up with the local bus operators' association, a necessary frustration from the very start, as it was the association's inability (if they ever really tried) to get their members' support that ultimately led to the project's downfall.

"I was bowled over by Curitiba, and have been a great proponent of its system ever since. I linked up there with Rikard Jonsson of Volvo, a Spanish-speaking 6-ft plus Swedish army reservist, who was to be my opposite number in Bogotá – and the ideal colleague in a sometimes rather frightening place – and Alan Cannell, a Manx-born transport consultant who had gone to Brazil as a young man, liked the girls, decided to stay, married one, and brought up a family there. Alan had been one of Lerner's acolytes, had helped develop the Curitiba system, and did all the hard work preparing our bid while Rikard, Oswaldo Schmitt from Volvo do Brasil and I made the rounds and tried to come up with a workable relationship with our new partners. As I have said, this was where our troubles started, for while the local operators knew they couldn't stay out of the process, the last thing they wanted was to give away any of their business to a bunch of gringos. We had the best scheme, we knew it was what Mayor Castro wanted and we won the tender with our proposal for a Curitiba-based network called Sistema Metrobús de Bogotá, but in the end we just couldn't put a consortium deal together and the plan collapsed. Metrobús is generally acknowledged to have been a vital precursor to the highly-successful Transmilénio scheme, in which this time the locals got to hold on to all their business. Metrobús had made them realize they had to embrace change (especially by moving to more economical higher-capacity vehicles) which was probably what Castro and then Mockus were really after right from the start.

"It was a hard slog trying to make any progress and often thoroughly demoralizing, but it was also an exciting place to be when you had the opportunity to make a huge change for the better in a major city. There were many surreal moments along the way like the time Brian Souter visited and we all went to a meeting in a posh office building. The rest of us were used to Bogotá by then but Brian became quite animated by the airport-style security and the sign saying *All firearms to be left here*. His imagination seemed to get the better of him during the meeting when he was sure that what the rest of us thought were backfires right outside were actually gunshots. He was right of course, as usual. There had

Curitiba's achievements impressed the Bogotá authorities who sought to replicate them. Once the authorities eventually came to terms with existing operators, this segregated Transmilenio busway system was successfully launched in December 2000 and has since expanded to a nine-line network carrying nearly 2 million passengers a day. (Alan Cannell)

been a bank robbery and a running gunfight as the perpetrators tried to escape. It was the only gunfire I heard in Bogotá in all the months I was there but that sort of thing seemed to follow Brian around!

"There was the time Keith Cochrane, then Stagecoach's Finance Director, visited. Those who knew Keith then will remember how impatient he always was, rushing around, even kicking lift doors if the lift wasn't quick enough to arrive. He also carried a ridiculously heavy briefcase that I could barely lift; I told him he'd soon have the long arms of an orang-utang if it got any heavier (he already had the red hair). I also warned him that the air was thin at 8,500 feet, and to take it easy but no sooner had he arrived than he dashed up two flights of stairs (with briefcase, of course) and almost collapsed in a heap at the top. He didn't have a heart attack, thankfully, but then had another narrow miss a few days later when Bogotá was hit by a 7.3 magnitude earthquake, whose epicentre was fortunately quite deep and some way from the city. I was near the hotel entrance and immediately felt it and dashed over to Keith, who was in the middle of one of his interminable phone calls. 'Out, out, quick!' I shouted, and then grabbed him and got him out. The whole place was shaking alarmingly, the road felt like wobbling jelly, and all the wires were swaying like mad. Luckily there was no damage nearby, but our Swedish colleagues were at the time renewing their business visas in the Swedish embassy and happened

to be in its so-called strong room, one of whose walls instantly cracked from top to bottom. We suffered after-shocks all week, including one in the airport departure lounge waiting for the BA flight; we were even more pleased than usual to be on our way home that time.

"Then there was the time we went to meet Colombia's President, Ernesto Samper, who was to become embroiled in a scandal about money provided by the Cali drugs cartel being used to finance his campaign. If the amount of military hardware at the Mayor's offices was daunting, especially in the hands of 18-year old recruits (the offices were right next to the Supreme Court which FARC guerrillas had previously blown up with heavy loss of life), its apparent absence at the President's Palace oddly seemed even more so. We were duly conveyed to the grand presence, had a perfectly pleasant and encouraging meeting and then somehow managed to get lost on the way out. We must have been pointed in the right direction but we weren't accompanied and ended up on a lower level in an anonymous corridor. I can't remember who was with me that day, but I'm not sure anyone's Spanish would have been good enough to deter a trigger-happy security guard. All turned out well with lots of smiles (there were always lots of smiles in Colombia) but for a moment it was the most frightening experience of my whole time in Bogotá.

"One Sunday we had a long-awaited trip out of town by steam train, with hundreds of happy families and a brass band, and a bang-up lunch at the other end, except that half-way there the Baldwin loco derailed and the trip came to an ignominious end. We'd arranged for a car to pick us up at the far end and so we walked back along the track to a village we'd just passed, and grabbed a taxi to our planned destination. There we brought the unwelcome news that hundreds of Sunday lunches would go uneaten but by goodness did we get wonderful service, eating until we could scarcely move. The train, and its huge load of passengers, eventually got back to Bogotá many hours later.

"Finally, there was the time the clock was stopped; this brings us back to Mockus. While the contract process was still ongoing, Castro's term as Mayor had ended and Mockus had been elected as his successor. An academic at Bogotá University, and best known at the time for baring his backside at a rally to show what he thought of his audience, he became mayor on 1st January 1995, where he continued to indulge in press-grabbing antics while getting serious about Bogotá's social and traffic problems. We

duly won the contract, which will have been no surprise to either Castro or Mockus, who were clearly rather more ready than Britain has still yet been to embrace affordable bus-based solutions, and signed up just before Castro left office at the end of 1994. Unfortunately, although we'd won we were still arguing with our partners, and an early deadline was fast approaching by which time we had to make various financial commitments. If the deadline was missed, the contract would be void and the City would have to start all over again. Mockus as a result presided over an eleventh-hour meeting aimed at sorting things out.

"The meeting was interminable, in Spanish, with virtually nothing translated. As I recall, it lasted 18 hours – it was one of many very long meetings. The deadline was midnight, and as it approached we weren't making much if any headway. I looked nervously at the clock every few minutes as midnight grew closer but no one else seemed unduly alarmed. Poker-faced brinkmanship, I thought, not having much of a clue about what was being said. And then, at a minute to midnight, Mockus casually stood up, wandered to the clock – and stopped it. 'OK', he said, 'let's continue'. And so we did, until about 6am, by which time something had been cobbled together that would pass muster under Colombian law, and Mockus could start the clock again. We'd already learned that Colombian law was exceptionally complex, and seemed to be designed to let those with money wriggle out of it while entrapping gringos who thought laws were made to be abided by.

"Unfortunately it became increasingly obvious that there was a complete stalemate. By April 1995 the contract was effectively dead and we had no realistic option but to walk away. We should almost certainly have given up sooner. Bjorn Larsson, Volvo Bus boss at the time, said to Rikard and myself near the end (having done all the hard work, Alan had by then disappeared on to more productive tasks elsewhere), 'The trouble with you guys is that you never know when to quit'. I don't think he meant it as a compliment, but we took it as one anyway.

"Mockus then immediately ordered work to begin on developing a deliverable scheme, which just over five years later came to fruition as Transmilénio. Brian always thereafter seemed pleased that I'd agreed to go, given Colombia's reputation but I don't remember it being put quite like that! We were probably both even more pleased he hadn't had to pay any ransoms. I wouldn't have missed the experience for anything."

THREE CLOSE CALLS

Sometimes things don't go according to plan and then quick thinking or good fortune determines a successful outcome. The following are three very different examples of such situations.

At the height of the troubles in Northern Ireland, Walter Heubeck had the unenviable task of managing Ulsterbus in Belfast. Walter had one enormous advantage in this tinderbox situation; he was German and was therefore probably the only person who was trusted by both sides. I met Walter when he came to Sunderland in 1975. Walter told us how the paramilitary organisations had taken to hijacking his buses which they then used to block the road with, and how they would set them ablaze. It made good visual publicity and, if they were lucky, the Royal Ulster Constabulary could be drawn into an ambush. Walter's problem was that while the government would compensate him for his burnt out buses he was unable to replace their Autoslot ticket machines as the Bell Punch Company had stopped making them.

They never used to throw anything away in Sunderland and had kept thirty redundant autoslot machines in the Wheatsheaf stores, hence the reason for Walter's visit. He treated us to lunch before his return with the machines to Stranraer for the ferry to Larne.

Over lunch he told us of one bizarre occasion when he had successfully managed to swap one hijacked vehicle for another. While the government paid Walter compensation for the loss of his burnt out vehicles, the money he received was an average price for each incident. Thus on one occasion when a driver radioed in to report his bus had been hijacked, Walter decided he had to intervene. The bus concerned was less than a year old and Walter immediately went to the radio control room and ordered the driver to put the terrorists

Here relegated to training duties, this 43-seat Alexander (Belfast) bodied Bristol LH was one of a batch of 100 bought new by Ulsterbus in 1973 for rural services. (Roy Marshall)

on the radio. The site of the incident was only five minutes away from the depot and he told them that if they could wait a few minutes, he would swap their new bus for an old one! The deal was done and Walter jumped into the cab of the oldest bus in the depot, drove it through the armed Police lines and made the exchange. He told us that the paramilitaries were quite accommodating; they just wanted a bus to torch and weren't too bothered about its pedigree. On this occasion at least, he was able to make a profit out of the incident. Talking later to Ted Hesketh, Walter's successor, Ted told me that only Walter could have pulled this off at that time.

A terrorist attack of a very different kind occurred on 7th July 2005 when four suicide bombers attacked the London Transport system. Three bombs went off on the Underground, but the fourth was on a Stagecoach London bus in Tavistock Square. Thirteen people died in the bus attack and the incident shocked everybody at Stagecoach. Stagecoach Cheltenham training staff reflected that their new drivers were not well prepared for a bomb incident and set out to rectify the position with a training session on how to deal with suspicious packages. To add authenticity to the exercise they constructed an impressive

dummy shoebox bomb with accompanying wires and an alarm clock to add realism to the training programme.

It was August 2007, not long after the waters had receded from the July floods and the device was placed on the training vehicle. Except on this occasion the normal training vehicle was being serviced so a Dennis Dart SLF service bus was used instead. Exercise complete, the trainer and his trainees repaired to the canteen for a cuppa. On return, the Dart had disappeared to take up service A between Prestbury and GCHQ Benhall via Cheltenham Town Centre. As soon as the bus left Cheltenham High Street heading for GCHQ, a passenger came running down to the driver to report a bomb on the back seat.

The driver immediately evacuated the bus and called 999 reporting what he had been told. The police quickly arrived, inspected the vehicle and promptly called for the bomb squad.

Stagecoach Newcastle took delivery of 10 Designline Olympus 29-seat turbine electric buses in July 2005. Purchased for the Nexus QuayLink contract, 61005 is seen here on the Quayside with the famous Tyne Bridge in the background. The vehicles' sophisticated electronics proved less than reliable and when the contract passed to Go Ahead Northern, they were returned to the manufacturer who, following modification redeployed them to California. (Nexus)

Cheltenham town centre was soon brought to a standstill with the area cleared, cordons set-up and premises evacuated. Cheltenham had never before seen a robot climb onto a bus and apprehensive looking police officers were pacing the streets clearly thinking that this was a terrorist attack on GCHQ. News of the lockdown reached the depot and the driver trainer wanted to know what all the fuss was about. When told, the colour drained from his cheeks and he exclaimed, "Oh my God, I left my shoebox on that bus!" It was left to his boss, Sholto Thomas, to apologise to an incredulous and increasingly annoyed Police Commander. It was too late to recover the shoe box as the army robot had already conducted a controlled obliteration of it in the street.

My third tale is of "the show must go on" genre. The Newcastle and Gateshead Quaysides are the north-east's highest profile redevelopment area. The Romans were the first to bridge the Tyne at this, its lowest, crossing point leading eventually to the development of Newcastle and Gateshead on its north and south banks. More recently, with commercial shipping retreating to North Shields ten miles downstream, the riverside and its warehouses fell into disuse and it wasn't until the Tyne & Wear Enterprise zone was created in 1981 that its fortunes began to reverse. Today, there is renewed activity with new Court buildings, warehouse conversions, modern office blocks, hotels, restaurants and apartments on the north bank. The eye-catching Sage Concert Halls and the Arts Galleries housed in the old Baltic Flour mill are situated on the south bank and the two quays are connected by the impressive Millennium footbridge, whose arch echoes that of the iconic Tyne Bridge some 250 metres upstream. The long running historic

rivalry between the Gateshead and Newcastle authorities ensured that the control room needed to enable the footbridge to rise, was duplicated with one installed at each end!

With the river in a gorge, its six main crossings are at all at high level, providing the direct road and rail routes between the two centres. With no prospects of commercial bus operation, the PTE was required by the PTA to come up with a package of services to feed the new developments from both Gateshead Metro in the south and Monument Metro to the north, dropping to the riverside and using the low level swing-bridge en route. This was going to be a prestige operation befitting the economic revival that the riverside regeneration represented to the Geordie nation. Government funding was secured and Stagecoach entered into the spirit of the project by offering to procure revolutionary buses which were electrically powered by eighty lead acid batteries topped up by an electronically controlled diesel turbine generator. Manufactured in New Zealand by Design Line, these low emission buses were going to cost around £250,000 each and the contract called for ten vehicles. A prototype was shipped to the UK in October 2004 and before arrival on Tyneside it was shown to a number of interested Authorities in the south of England. Kim Teasdale was responsible for the prototype's introductory tour and tells how this was far from plain sailing.

The visit to Winchester went well, as officials and councillors from Hampshire County Council rode the

Spirit of London was so named by London Mayor, Ken Livingstone. It was the first 76-seat Enviro 400 off the Alexander Dennis production line in December 2005 and replaced the Stagecoach bus lost at Tavistock Square in the 7/7 London bombings. It is seen here in March 2012 leaving Walthamstow Bus Station. (Julian Walker)

bus while Kim put the vehicle through its paces. However, as it was coming to the end of its test run Kim noticed the display panel was indicating that the turbine was failing. Once the dignitaries had departed Kim was able to inspect the turbine and the sophisticated diagnostics suggested that the instrument panel was right. Kim rang New Zealand. They carried out their own remote diagnostics and confirmed Kim's analysis. The turbine was kaput with a broken drive shaft. Still not to worry, they had one ready to be shipped air freight from Los Angeles and would divert that to Gatwick. Kim was relieved as next stop was Ramsgate where Secretary of State Alistair Darling was due to launch the new kick-start scheme in Thanet with Brian Souter and other dignitaries in attendance. The vehicle was winched on to its low-loader and set off for Kent. On arrival at the depot the demised turbine was removed in anticipation of the replacement unit arriving. The day before the launch Kim received news that the turbine was held up in Customs and was therefore going nowhere. He calculated that a fully charged set of batteries would get them round the test route, with a few minutes to spare, so the bus was plugged into the depot charging point right up to the last minute before departure.

The party boarded and remarked how quiet the ride was. Not surprising really when Kim was driving the bus in milk float mode. During the trip, Brian Souter suggested that when the demonstration run was competed, the Secretary of State should see how the bus worked with particular emphasis on showing him the turbine which, as only Kim knew, was currently lying on a wooden pallet back at the depot. Panic set in as Kim wondered how much longer he would be working for Stagecoach when Brian saw the void where the turbine should have been. As they neared completion of the test route, Brian suggested they should now go further and put the vehicle through its paces up a nearby hill, to which Alistair Darling readily agreed. They were both enjoying themselves, unlike Kim who now had an even greater sense of doom. However, as Kim set off in trepidation, one of Alistair Darling's entourage stepped in to remind the Minister that he was shortly scheduled to catch a particular train back to London. So Kim was instructed instead to take the party down to the station, a few hundred yards along the road; crisis over! As Kim remarked later it was a pretty close call, but his distinguished passengers, including his Chief Executive, were none the wiser – until now that is.

GOING FOR GOLD

One enduring memory of the London 2012 Olympics and Paralympics was the sight of British competitors giving media interviews within minutes of completing their events. Often overcome with emotion, they would invariably say that this was the culmination of four years hard work and, if they had won, how it had all been worthwhile, or conversely, if they had not, how devastated they were.

Hard work and meticulous planning extended to every aspect of the Games, not least the transport arrangements. London 2012 was billed as the public transport Games, since all but Olympic dignitaries in their chauffeured BMWs using the dedicated Olympic lanes, were obliged to visit most of the Olympic events by public transport. The numbers were big: 10 million spectators, 30 venues, 14,700 athletes and 21,000 media representatives, as well as 70,000 volunteers and 100,000 staff of transport and other contractors which all added up to the biggest movement of people for any event ever staged in the UK.

Planning began in July 2005, when London won the bid to host the 2012 Olympics. The responsibility to make it all happen rested with two separate bodies. The Olympic Delivery Authority (ODA) was charged with providing the infrastructure needed for the Games, including the means to get the spectators to and from the events. Meanwhile, the London Organising Committee of the Olympic and Paralympic Games (LOCOG) was responsible for staging the games themselves which included getting the athletes, the media and others to the right places at the right times. The ODA was publicly funded, while LOCOG's activities were to be largely funded by the private sector through sponsorship, broadcasting rights and merchandising.

I recall one early meeting with LOCOG representatives at the Confederation of Passenger Transport (CPT), the industry's trade association. Full of enthusiasm, the LOCOG people spelt out the scale of the transport requirement and invited us to provide the services it needed gratis, in return for allowing us to promote our own brands. Nobody present could see any commercial merit in this proposition and when LOCOG hinted that European operators would be only too willing to participate on these terms, the reaction around

Six days before the Official Opening Ceremony and the Olympic Transport network was already up and running. Heading northbound in an Olympic lane is a Translink 74-seat Wright Gemini Volvo B9TL, followed by an Arriva London 62-seat Wright Gemini DAF DB 250 and alongside a Brighton & Hove Irizar-bodied Scania coach. Meanwhile heading south is a Stagecoach Manchester 80-seat Alexander Dennis ALX 400. All identifying logos have been removed to meet strict LOCOG branding requirements. (Andy Izatt)

This is one of ten Stagecoach 33-seat Wrightbus StreetLites leading the support vehicles while the Olympic Torch was "in transit" through Pode Hole near Spalding on 4th July 2012. Bringing up the rear is one of two BuzzLine Van Hool Volvo T9Ls. Vehicles for the torch relay were all re-liveried for the 70 day tour, during which 8000 torchbearers carried the Olympic flame in the course of its 8000 mile tour of the British Isles. (Andy Izatt)

First Group held the Olympic Delivery Authority (ODA) contract for spectator transport to games venues. Unlike LOCOG, the ODA had no restrictions preventing First from promoting its own brand. This frequent service was for the rowing events at Eton Dorney. Looking very tidy is a departing 75-seat Plaxton Dennis Trident, initially with First Capital but now refurbished for provincial use. Approaching is a 2012 75-seat Alexander Dennis Enviro 400. (Andy Izatt)

the table was very much "they are welcome to do so". However, LOCOG soon realised that it would have to buy its bus services and in due course it and the ODA invited tenders for the bus and coach services they planned to deliver, in both cases contracting one operator to plan and manage the transport activities through framework contracts. They then awarded further contracts to operators to provide vehicles and drivers to work to their approved specifications and the managing operator's instructions.

Transport for London (TfL), as the host transport authority, had a special responsibility to keep London moving and to augment its own rail and bus services to carry spectators, volunteers and contractors staff to the Olympic Park and central London events. It also provided free travel cards to spectators and those involved in Games delivery, including the volunteers. TfL mounted a very effective campaign to persuade its regular passengers to keep out of London and off its transport

system for the duration of the Olympics. This proved so successful that during the events central London traders were bemoaning a loss of business. Bus services which passed near Games venues were augmented and in all 250 extra buses were added to the contracted London bus network's daily peak vehicle requirement. TfL also kept a strategic reserve of 50 "hot spares", buses with drivers, at North Greenwich, which could be called upon by any of the parties should the need arise. Apart from its bus and rail responsibilities, TfL developed web-based advice for freight route and delivery planning, which was updated hourly as part of its wider responsibility for strategic highways management. All credit must be given to it, not only getting its bus service levels right, but also for ensuring that its traffic management of the 109 mile Olympic Route Network with its 31 miles of Olympic Games lanes was beyond reproach. Indeed, it did this sufficiently well that the much predicted Olympic gridlock never materialized anywhere, at any time.

Stagecoach's temporary Beckton premises for the Olympic Games held 600 buses with nearby parking for a further 120. It was thought to be the largest bus depot in Europe. 920 bus staff were billeted on the Fred Olsen line cruise ship MS Braemar. Under maritime jurisdiction, all personnel had to go through security control housed in the tent (right foreground) each time they boarded the vessel. The second cruise ship (to the rear) accommodated the G4S Olympics security personnel. (Andrew Thompson)

The ODA framework contract for dedicated spectator travel, including park and ride, shuttle connections, accessible transport and coach parking, was awarded to First Group. Meanwhile, LOCOG awarded its framework contract for the delivery of the athletes, technical officials, dignitary and media transport to Stagecoach, with both groups setting up new companies with new Operators licences to deliver their commitments. With Traffic Commissioner's approval, both operators ran their compliant operations as special regular services and gained European Commission clearance to manually record drivers' hours on vehicles not fitted with tachographs. In addition, Stagecoach operated LOCOG's torch relay contract with a fleet of ten vehicles accompanying the torch as it toured the British Isles and Arriva held a LOCOG contract to provide 440 coaches to meet its Coach Charter Programme.

To deliver the ODA's framework agreement First Group held a 320 vehicle "O" licence for its temporary Barking depot facility. Reading

Transport was then contracted to clean, wash, fuel and park vehicles. As well as 200 of its own vehicles, some 637 others were contracted to meet its obligations. These included 118 coaches on direct links to the Olympic Park (which could be booked on its dedicated website), 88 buses on shuttles between railway stations and Olympic venues and 466 vehicles working park-and-ride services to the Olympic Park and a number of other Games sites. Accessible transport shuttles, using 165 wheelchair-adapted minibuses were contracted from ECT Group, the community transport charity which began life as Ealing Community

Transport. It brought in vehicles from a host of community transport operators. First Group also contracted operators to provide park and ride services to the Olympic football venues, including all seven fixtures at Hampden Park in Glasgow. First's contract drivers wore ODA uniforms and had to complete a tailored CPC course as part of their gaining the ODA "One Team Accreditation".

The LOCOG framework agreement required Stagecoach to manage two temporary bus depots. The media and technical officials' services depot accommodated 600 buses and together with its overflow 120-space bus parking area was reckoned to be the largest in Europe. Meanwhile the athletes' services depot accommodated 400 buses. To deliver these services LOCOG contracted 37 operators to provide the 1000 buses needed to cover its specified operations. 500 of these were provided by Stagecoach, which it manned with 1143 volunteer drivers drawn from all but one of its garages. This exercise required careful advance planning, including the rescheduling of drivers' holiday rosters and PCV annual tests so that its local bus services could still be maintained for the duration. Given its size, the organization needed to run a 600 bus depot also needed careful thought, and the company opted for a divisional approach comprising separate teams, each of which was responsible for around 100 vehicles and their drivers.

As Stagecoach was to deliver all of the LOCOG services for athletes, media and technical officials, every driver from each of the operators completed a Stagecoach designed, LOCOG approved, Olympics CPC course, which included Stagecoach operating procedures and defect reporting systems. One Stagecoach driver from Orkney also enjoyed the novel experience of driving a bus on a dual carriageway for the first time in his life.

As part of its framework contract, Stagecoach also scheduled LOCOG's requirements for its 410 separate bus services, the timetables for which changed daily. A team of schedulers worked through each night to produce daily instructions by 6am from input which LOCOG were due to supply by 4pm the afternoon before, but which on occasions arrived much later – in one case at 3.30am. The company also carried out route risk assessments on LOCOG's behalf, which included testing 12-metre vehicles on every route. LOCOG's scheduling specification required that each service should operate at 30 minute frequencies over the period it was

required and that departures were timed at the same minutes past the hour from both termini. This requirement, which was made to ensure that all the sporting teams were treated equally, was favoured instead of higher frequency services for high demand events and it led to large numbers of duplicates, with LOCOG specifying a requirement for nineteen on one occasion. Following requests from the broadcasters, fifteen minute frequencies were soon introduced on some services provided for the media and technical officials.

In order to protect its sponsors, LOCOG imposed very specific non-disclosure agreements on its contractors preventing any promotion of their involvement. These included LOCOG brand protection and the suppression of operators' brand identities. Some interesting discussions took place about the removal of manufacturers' brand names from tyres and the re-trimming of seats to remove identifiable logo patterns, neither of which could be accommodated within LOCOG budgets. For obvious reasons, LOCOG's initial desire to remove legal lettering displaying the operator's name on the sides of vehicles was resisted. However the temporary coverage of some manufacturers' badges and all operator trading names and logos on vehicle exteriors were all undertaken as part of LOCOG's contractual requirements.

With so many people descending on East London for such a short period, accommodation was an early consideration in the LOCOG planning process. Originally, it was intended that most contracted bus staff from outside London would be housed in student halls of residence. As planning progressed, some of this accommodation was re-allocated to the media and games officials. Consequently, some 920 drivers had to be transferred to a cruise ship after operations had begun; this was moored alongside the larger of the two bus depots. While the floating accommodation was undeniably good, it created problems of its own since the ship was under maritime jurisdiction and security included passport-style checks each time anyone boarded the vessel. Further, when one of the crew contracted chicken pox and the Port of London Authority was duly notified, it was suggested that all passengers and crew should be immediately quarantined. Fortunately, this proposition, which would have brought much of the Olympic Games to a dramatic halt, was discounted.

Games security was always first priority after the events in Munich and because of continuing international terrorism. The security contractor, G4S, hit the headlines only two weeks before the Games started when it acknowledged that it would be unable to meet its manpower commitments.

This resulted in the army being drafted in to assist and the House of Commons Home Affairs Select Committee subjecting the company's chief executive to a ritual humiliation. LOCOG's transport contracts were placed under the strictest scrutiny, none more so than the vehicles conveying the athletes. Access to the depot was tightly controlled and every flap on every bus was secured with tamper-proof tape. Under-vehicle inspections with mirrors and sniffer dog vehicle checks were undertaken and drivers were not permitted to allow anyone to board or alight between termini. You can therefore imagine the consternation when, only two days before the opening ceremony, a coach scheduled to be carrying dignitaries caught fire. There was a real concern that this was some sort of failed terrorist attack and until investigations indicated that the cause was an electrical fault, alarm bells were ringing everywhere. Another security issue arose when it was found that the security wipes of steering wheels undertaken to detect traces of explosives were sometimes proving positive. Again alarm bells rang until the source was traced to the cleaning agent used on buses from one particular contractor's depot.

Maintaining 1000 buses, even for a relatively short period, also required careful planning, particularly when the vehicles were being provided by so many operators. To meet "O" licence requirements, each vehicle was subjected to a Stagecoach inspection on arrival before it could enter service. This produced some wide-ranging results, which for the sake of one or two operators' reputations must remain confidential. Another unnamed operator had three times more breakdowns than anyone else! Initial discussions with LOCOG focused on providing temporary tented maintenance facilities but the practicalities of constructing and moving 4½-metre high canvas doors and the 7-metre headroom needed for a double-decker standing on a raised lift, proved challenging. The issue was compounded by the need to ensure that the lifts themselves would be standing on level surfaces capable of safely supporting up to 15 tonnes. The conundrum remained unresolved until Stagecoach was able to offer a recently vacated East London bus garage which became the temporary maintenance hub for all of the LOCOG contracted buses under Stagecoach control.

So how did it all pan out? After the G4S fiasco, the media was looking for things to go wrong in the early days. They weren't disappointed when on the first day of athlete airport transfers one driver missed the turning to the Olympics Park and took his passengers on an additional twenty minute excursion. To his credit, Lord Coe, the LOCOG chairman, defended the operators by pointing out that just one in one hundred drivers had erred and London Mayor, Boris Johnson, made light of it by pointing out that the passengers had experienced a bonus tour of his "wonderful city".

Given the number of operators and staff involved, and the fact that they were all being brought together for the first time in unfamiliar surroundings working to one operator's procedures, the achievement was remarkable. Drivers loved the experience, some even commenting that they couldn't believe that they were being paid for what they were doing. When their time came to leave, some two-thirds of them asked if they could stay longer than their allotted period. For the supervisors and managers, however, the main Olympics were extremely challenging. They were managing a 24/7 operation with up to 150 buses working through the night for over six weeks and many of them voluntarily worked eighteen hour days until the necessary extra support was drafted in. With so many vehicle movements, keeping track of all of the buses was not easy, even with the use of an automated vehicle location system. After the first day of 24 hour operations, it was suddenly discovered that no fewer than 46 buses had been lost! Panic set in until it was realized 40 minutes later that some night bus drivers had left their vehicles at the Olympic Park, an unintended consequence of scheduling 28 hour days. This was one of those heart-stopping incidents which everyone laughed about – but only much later after the dust had settled.

Before then however, the operators had to cope with their most logistically challenging day. On paper this was the third day of Games competition but in practice it turned out to be the day after the Olympics closing ceremony. Transport after the event was required until 2am, but what was not expected was the volume of athletes' service duplication to Heathrow, which was needed extensively through the night from 1.30am onwards. Add to the mix, the requirement to decommission 370 buses and disembark 920 people from their cruise-ship lodgings, 300 of whom had to then be re-housed in other LOCOG arranged accommodation; it all made for a very long day.

By comparison, the Paralympics were less demanding, but still required meticulous attention to detail given the additional need to ensure that the athletes' buses and the separately contracted logistics trucks carrying their equipment arrived in the same places at the same time. There was also a requirement to convert in a fortnight, no fewer than 250 Stagecoach and 20 other single-deck buses each to carry six wheelchairs, all of which were signed off by VOSA in a fast track approvals process. Nine of the ten torch relay vehicles were used again, but re-liveried to promote the Paralympics brand. Operations went well, although on one occasion considerable energies had to be diverted to re-uniting a prosthetic leg with its rightful owner after it had apparently been left on one of the vehicles.

Overall, the Olympics were a job very well done by all the bus and coach operators involved. Mark Yexley, CPT President, summed it all up when he was quoted in the trade press saying; "Everyone who has taken part will be able to walk away with a deep sense of pride in doing their bit towards such a big success story". Yet the industry has not been widely applauded for its achievements. Comments on BBC Radio 4 included observations such as "at least the transport worked", which was typical of the nation's reaction. Should we have expected more? Probably not – the reality is that we are expected to deliver in the same way that we expect the light to come on when we flick the switch, or the water to flow when we turn on the tap. Had we not done so, then we would have been pilloried – but Olympic bus services that did what it said on the tin, just like any other bus service, were taken for granted.

There has also been much talk about the Olympics legacy and maybe there is one for the bus industry too. The biggest enduring benefit was that many thousands of people rode on buses for the first time since their childhood. They will have noticed that the vehicles and the comfort of their ride have improved beyond recognition and that drivers were both courteous and friendly – something they will hopefully not forget when they ponder whether they should give the bus a try back home.

Shelley Usher, Assistant Operations Manager at Walkergate for Stagecoach Newcastle, worked at Beckton Depot throughout the Olympics Games. Her sister sent her a moonpig Greetings card bearing this image. Shelley installed it as a poster on the control room wall throughout her stay. (moonpig.com)

TIME TO SAY GOODBYE

It is often said that the only certainties in our lives are taxes and death. This final chapter concerns three bus industry funerals at which I and many others were privileged to pay our final respects to the deceased.

Alan Patey

Alan Patey was a driver at the Busways, Byker Depot in Newcastle who tragically died in service. On only the third day of deregulation, 28th October 1986, he was driving service 21 on Scotswood Road towards Throckley that afternoon. Alan's bus was in collision with an HGV laden with concrete blocks travelling in the opposite direction. Alan and two passengers died that day, while 40 more passengers were injured, some seriously.

Fatal bus accidents are devastating for the family of the employees concerned, their work colleagues and their employers, just as they are for any passengers or third parties involved. This accident was made even worse by the intervention of an opportunistic Labour MP who, within hours, was using Parliamentary privilege to claim in the chamber of the House of Commons that these deaths were the result of deregulation. Nothing could have been more hurtful to his grieving wife and children. His colleagues and the company were incensed. Service 21 had not changed at deregulation and, at that time, there were no new competing services on the route. It transpired that Alan had been on time and that the HGV had crossed the white line and ploughed into the offside front of the bus, ripping through the cab and much of the offside. Some months later at the inquest, it was established that the HGV had hit a pot hole causing its driver to lose control of his vehicle. Alan was one of those model employees who can be found in every bus depot in the land. He was a family man who came to work and did his job. He was never off sick and he never reported late. He didn't have a disciplinary record and he never attracted passenger complaints; the sort of employee who is the backbone of every bus operation. We wrote from the company to the MP demanding an apology to the family but, as we might have expected, received no reply. He had made his political point and he didn't care one jot about their feelings.

Alan's funeral was held at North Shields Crematorium and I shall never forget walking solemnly and silently behind his family as we followed the coffin through the guard of honour made up of two lines comprising 150 of his colleagues smartly dressed in their driver's uniforms. Nothing needed to be said, Alan was a thoroughly decent ordinary busman who was respected by all.

Nick Painter

Nick Painter was a solicitor who, when I first met him, worked for the Simpson Curtis Partnership in Leeds. He had been recommended to us by our accountants, Arthur Andersen, as a specialist in commercial law and the buying and selling of bus businesses. Nick had seen the opportunities emerging when the NBC companies were privatized and already had a good reputation in the bus industry by the time Busways was moving from PTA ownership into management and employee ownership in 1989.

Nick was no city slicker being somewhat dishevelled in appearance, even when sporting a new suit. He was a serious smoker with an infectious laugh and unusual working hours. I soon learnt that ringing him before 10.30am was a fool's errand but he would answer his office phone until at least 7.30pm most evenings. Nick knew his onions and had also built up a formidable knowledge of the bus industry by the time I got to know him. I recall the completion meeting for our purchase of the Busways Company which was held in Newcastle's Station Hotel. For those not conversant with the acquisition process, there needs to be a series of shareholders and directors meetings in a particular order to complete the legal niceties. Imagine then a roomful of people, including lawyers and accountants for the PTA, the directors of the new Busways Company, the trustees of the employee benefit trust, accountants for the company, lenders to the company, a merchant banker's representative and of course, Nick and his secretary. As often happens on these occasions, there were some late changes tabled to the sale and purchase agreement and in amongst all the hubbub, Nick lay face down on the floor quickly scanning through reams of documentation which had just been handed to him. How he wasn't trodden on or tripped over, I will never know.

We used Nick's services again when the management and employees sold Busways to Stagecoach in 1994. Before the process was finalized we held a meeting with Stagecoach representatives at the offices of Noble Grossart in Edinburgh to conclude some of the remaining details. This time there were only six or seven of us, one of whom was Nick. When we broke for lunch, Nick checked his mobile text messages and advised us that unfortunately he had been sacked at 11am that morning but his professional indemnity insurance meant he could continue to represent us, if we so wished. Our answer was an unequivocal yes. By 5pm our meeting was finished and all had been agreed to both parties' satisfaction. Nick again checked his mobile for messages and announced that he had just been reinstated. When we asked for an explanation, Nick advised us that he and five of his colleagues, together with their secretaries, had that morning advised the Simpson Curtis partners that they were leaving to set up another practice, Garretts, which was a new legal venture sponsored by Arthur Andersen. The partners immediate reaction had been to dismiss them all but fortunately one of the defecting solicitors was an employment law specialist who had advised the Simpson Curtis partners that such action was unlawful; he had then sat down and negotiated an orderly exit for the twelve of them.

Nick's services didn't come cheap by provincial standards but were excellent value for what he did. He was also one of those lawyers who would happily give advice freely over the phone at any time without putting it on the clock, preferring instead to recover his costs on the bigger jobs. This he maintained, even when his later employers DLA Piper discouraged such practices.

Nick died at the age of 48, whilst snorkelling on a family holiday. His funeral was held at Ilkley Parish Church on 17th September 2007. The church was packed, with family and business associates from the law, accountancy, merchant banking and particularly the bus industry. During the service we heard more of his wicked sense of humour. Nick, who originated from Swansea, came from a professional family but he would tell people that his father was a miner and that as a youngster he would go down to the pit at the end of his father's shift and would lead home the family's pit pony, which was called Eric. As Nick's coffin left the church, the whole congregation burst into spontaneous applause – an unusual, but nevertheless very fitting tribute to the man who had been at the heart of the sale and purchase of so many bus company privatizations and mergers.

Peter Huntley

Peter died on 19th February 2012 aged 55, whilst hill walking in the Lake District with a colleague. He was training for his forthcoming trek to the North Pole when he tripped and fell 500 feet. Peter was known throughout the industry, having co-founded the Bus Business publication in 1986 and the TAS consultancy partnership in 1994. His route into the industry was somewhat unusual as he had left the London rat race with his then wife to try his hand at self-sufficiency as a Highland crofter. When that failed, he joined Highland Regional Council and became involved in public transport co-ordination, before moving to Lancashire as public transport co-ordinator. Peter's energy, enthusiasm and fearless determination to "tell it how it is" won him many admirers, and a few enemies, amongst the bus fraternity. Brian Souter, who firmly believes that management should manage and not pass their responsibilities to consultants, once told Peter that he didn't hold with consultants, but if he had to have one, then it would be him. Peter further enhanced his reputation when, in 2006, he was appointed to the post of Managing Director of Go North East (GNE), so that he could put his consultant's theories into practice. In his five years with that Company he completely reorganized the business and its image. The affection in which he was held by his staff is captured by this posthumous tribute from one employee on his justgiving website. "You were the first managing director I had met that was willing to meet and respond to staff concerns. You brought innovation and colour to the North East bus industry. You were an inspiration to us all at GNE and will be sadly missed".

Peter's funeral at Preston Crematorium was packed with over 150 colleagues and acquaintances from every corner of the bus industry. He supported no fewer than 15 charities and during the ceremony it was revealed that he was also a guerrilla gardener, planting thousands of bulbs in highway verges around the country. Peter's short temper and total lack of empathy for things mechanical was ably described by his son, Dan, who told us that as a child he recalled the family car refusing to start on one occasion. Rather than lift the bonnet to try to solve the problem, Peter had resorted to kicking the car tyres and shouting at the vehicle, with words that repeatedly doubted its parentage. As we came to the end of the service Dan concluded his tribute with words he was sure his father would have uttered in the situation we all now found ourselves. They were: "Stop fannying about and b***** off!"

And so we did, to reconvene in a nearby village hall where Peter's family had kindly arranged refreshments for us all.

AND FINALLY . . . MODEL BUSES

No book intent on capturing the spirit of the bus industry would be complete without mention of the army of collectors and enthusiasts who make the industry their hobby. Every bus operator, past and present, has its devotees, many of whom become experts in their chosen subject. David Thrower has a particular interest in London's buses of the '50s and '60s. His full-sized preserved vehicle collection comprises 2 RTs, 1 RTL, 1 RF and 1 RML, which can often be seen at Rallies and Bus Gatherings around the country. He also has a collection of over 400 1:50 scale model London buses. 300 of his fleet are RTs, RTLs and RTWs, mainly of Solido and Corgi manufacture, while twenty have been hand-built by Tony Howard. The balance includes 45 Routemasters and an assortment of RLHs, RFs, GSs and ancillary fleet vehicles. The accompanying pictures capture a small sample of David's model fleet on display at a recent event.

David's line-up of London Country Bus Services (LCBS) model RTs, seen lower right, typically reflects the fleet in the early 1970s. London Transport's Home Counties network of green bus services and its Green Line operations were transferred by statute to the National Bus Company on 1st January 1970. NBC was dealt a poor hand which included a loss making business, no cash, no central works and 484 16-20 year old RTs, representing two-thirds of the LCBS fleet. The last RT was withdrawn in 1978. (David Thrower, all)